The Relevance of Bliss

The Relevance of Bliss

A Contemporary Exploration
of Mystic Experience

Nona Coxhead

St. Martin's Press
New York

Library of Congress Cataloging in Publication Data

Coxhead, Nona.
    The relevance of bliss.

    Bibliography: p.
    1. Mysticism—Psychology.   2. Experience (Religion)
3. Ecstasy.   I. Title
BL625.C69   1986   291.4′2   86-17716
ISBN 0-312-67055-9 (pbk.)

First published in Great Britain by Wildwood House Ltd.

First U.S. Edition

10 9 8 7 6 5 4 3 2 1

Contents

Acknowledgements

The author wishes to express her thanks and appreciation to the many kind and cooperative people who have contributed their valuable ideas to this book: Dr. Peter Fenwick, Dr. Richard Petty, Prof. David Bohm, Tom Sensky, Dr. Jonathon Meads, Warren Kenton, Peter Russell, Fred Alan Wolf, Stanley Krippner, C. Maxwell Cade, Andrew Duncan, Hazel Guest, Dr. Rupert Sheldrake, Geoffrey Read, Margot Grey; and to Glen Schaefer, Fritjof Capra, Gary Zukav, Joseph Campbell, Jacob Needleman, Sir Alister Hardy, David Hay, Dr. Stanislav Grof, R.D. Laing, John Lilly, Gopi Krishna, Paramahansa Yogananda, Swami Muktananda, Arthur J. Deikman, Walter Pahnke, Alan Watts and F.C. Happold for their personal or publisher's permission to quote from their written work (see the Bibliography for details of publishers, places and dates of publication); also to the *New York Times* for permission to quote from the Andrew Greeley-William McCready poll *'Are We a Nation of Mystics?'*, to the publishers of *Mysticism: Spiritual Quest or Psychic Disorder* for excerpts from the *Group for the Advancement of Psychiatry* report, *The Wrekin Trust* for permission to quote from lectures given at their annual *Mystics and Scientists* Conferences at Winchester, to the editors of *Brain/Mind Bulletin*, *Re-Vision Journal*, *The International Journal of Parapsychology*, *Science of Mind* magazine, *Journal of Nervous and Mental Disease*.

'The religious man believes, the mystic knows'
— William James

Introduction

To explore the subject of mysticism is an immense proposition. Not only is its literature vast, scholarly and profound, but in constant process of enlargement and elaboration. As for mystic experience, the range of types and interpretations is as wide and varied as Man's individual beliefs, about himself, about God, about the nature of reality.

Happily, it is not my intention here to enlarge on mysticism *per se*, or to attempt to encompass the myriad degrees and forms of what may be broadly considered mystic experience.

Rather, while gratefully acknowledging existent mystic studies as the source of my observations and historical facts, I direct this exploration into allied territory, one particular kind of experience and its relevance to contemporary life, to humanity-at-large.

I have chosen to symbolise this singular experience with the term 'Bliss', because this is its most-often quoted characteristic, and at the risk of association with more frivolous connotations, have for the same reason used it as my title.

The experience itself is repeatedly defined by those who have had it, the 'mystics' themselves, in records as old as history, as 'impossible to mistake', as a 'shift' of perception and feeling so overpoweringly 'illuminating' that it cannot be confused with any other state of mind or consciousness. There is a sense of total transformation and transcendence into a higher realm of being, a merging into that which is indisputably benign and loving, that brings with it a 'knowing' that all is good, right, as it should be, a great glow of peace and joy and 'oneness', 'an absolute,' 'a supreme bliss'.

Of course there is no way to prove this experience exists, except by having it, but the body of evidence over the course of many centuries of spiritual accounts is surely as well-grounded as any phenomenon studied by science. It has always struck me as extraordinary that it should be overlooked, almost singularly left out of all investigative modern research. It is as if by ignoring it, it would simply evaporate, or better still, be written off as a phenomenon of religious hysteria.

Considering the climate of the times when most of the recorded saints and famous mystics flourished, were revered, listened to, based teachings and spiritual systems on the content of their mystic transport, this might have been a credible theory were it not for more recent anthologies presenting the mystic experience of people with no aspirations to be monks or nuns, to whom the experience simply 'happened'.

Having been mystically inclined myself since a child, with a persisting tendency to bursts of ecstatic joy, wonder, love of some invisible and immanent presence – which, as worldly matters took precedence subsided into a vague unverbalised awareness – I have felt an increasing urgency to do what I have done in this book: bring the evidence out into the light and into review, including the speculations of current psychology and science.

Among the first questions I wanted to ask were: Are those who have been called 'mystics' really a special breed, set apart from the rest of us? Do we have to be spiritually 'talented' or gifted, a higher, more advanced kind of human being? Or, at the least, must one be 'predisposed' to religious experience in order for it to occur?

My suspicion was that the answer was no, that we are all incipient mystics, but I had no wish to make any such claim. Well-aware of the views of psychoanalysts, that had put a definite blight on associating oneself with things mystic for fear of being classified as mentally unstable, even seriously ill, I began my own research with objective caution.

I gathered together some recent statistical studies that showed the incidence of mystic experience in a sample of the population both in the U.K. and in the U.S., I compared mystic experience in the East with mystic experience in the West, and I advertised for contemporary experiences from people who would agree to being named and make additional personal comment.

I thought these would be hard to find. So large was the response, however, that I had to cancel my advertising, my main effort being to sort out the nature of the experiences. I decided to eliminate some excellent examples because they contained elements, like visions, voices, images or occult undertones, that were not directly relevant to my particular approach since I wanted to focus on the 'Bliss' experience in isolation. I was astonished to learn how many people had had these experiences, and how willing, almost eager most of them were to speak of them: only about four responders insisted upon anonymity, and two of these changed their minds as they gained better understanding of my purpose.

In this exploration, then, many of these examples will illustrate certain aspects of what might be called an extension of mystic data: for although the repetitive element may not lend itself to hard science, it can be considered a 'soft' science – as David Bohm, the eminent theoretical physicist has said: 'The immeasurable is the primary and independent source of all reality . . . Measure is a secondary and dependent aspect of this reality.'

In order to clarify the components of mystic experience that lent themselves to the statistical approach, I also collected a substantial quantity of what both writers and mystics have considered the 'typology' of the 'flash of illumination' experience. John Ferguson, for instance, in the *Encyclopedia of Mysticism*, lists these characteristics, quoting W.T. Stace:

1. Unity (a) External: a sense of cosmic oneness
          (b) Internal: fading of ego into a state of pure awareness
2. Transcendence of time and space
3. Positive sensations: joy, bliss, love, peace
4. Sense of the numinous (pertaining to a divinity)
5. Sense of certitude: the reality of the mystical experience
6. Paradox. So in the *Isa Upanishad* (5) [one of the sacred Hindu texts]
          It moves. It does not move.
          It is far. It is near.
          It is within the whole universe.
          It is outside it.
7. Ineffability
8. Transience: the experience does not last
9. Resultant change of attitude and behaviour.

And Raynor C. Johnson, whose *Watcher on the Hill* and *The Imprisoned Splendour* include the mystical experiences of many 'ordinary' men and women of today, reports:

1. Those who have had the more profound type of mystical experiences, no matter in what age or to what race or creed they have belonged, tell us the same fundamental things: The sense of separateness vanished in an all-embracing unity, there is certain knowledge of immortality,

there is an enormously enhanced appreciation of values, and there is knowledge that at the heart of the universe is Joy and Beauty.
2. Those who have known such an experience are always profoundly impressed by its significance as a revelation of truth. There is from then onwards, not the satisfaction of an intellectual answer to life's ultimate questions, but a serenity born of the knowledge that all is well, and that the secret purpose of the universe is good beyond all telling.'

Also, Sir Alister Hardy, the distinguished British zoologist, author, and founder of the Religious Research Unit in Oxford, suggests these overlapping elements:

'Sense of joy, happiness, well-being, peace, new strength in oneself, awe, reverence, wonder, clarity, enlightenment, exaltation, harmony, order, timelessness, unity, protection, love, bliss.'

After exploring the nature of the experience, I also include questions regarding two types: the 'spontaneous' experience, which is simply 'triggered-off' in some completely unexpected and involuntary way and the type which is 'induced' by some means, such as meditation of various kinds, drugs, fasting, dervish dancing, fervent prayer, etc. I ask what, if any, the differences are in ultimate effect and ultimate value.

Rounding out the exploration from every possible angle, the book contains a broad spectrum of hypotheses of experts in a wide range of fields as to *what actually* takes place or *happens* in a mystical experience. The viewpoints of physics, biology, neurophysiology, psychology, psychoanalysis, theology, philosophy, medicine and biofeedback are included, as well as many others.

Finally, having researched, absorbed and hopefully digested all these ideas and findings, I have my 'author's say' as to what I have concluded from my own personal point of view: all readers are invited to do the same.

If this exploration succeeds in focusing the light of objective as well as subjective inquiry, raises sharper questions, results in a deeper, closer appraisal of the relevance of Bliss, then it will have served its purpose.

1
Bliss as History

'To study the mystic experience one must turn initially to material that appears unscientific, is couched in religious terms, and seems completely subjective...' – Arthur J. Deikman, (*Psychiatry*, 1966)

A contemporary view of mystic experience implies a base of historical reference from which is gained perspective for the new. To provide this with brevity must do such a far-reaching subject considerable injustice; but on the other hand, it does not even seem to have been achieved at length. For what takes shape from many hundreds of studies and analyses of mystic experience, who the mystics were, what they believed and taught down the centuries, in the East and in the West, is more of a generic than a chronological history. One learns much about mystics as a distinguishable class of humanity, of the classifiable elements of their experience, and of their shared aspirations and goals, but one does not gain a progressive record of their existence and development in time and place.

It is, therefore, only safe to generalise, to note that the 'mystic element' can be traced in records of all primitive religions. It is present in most of the Eastern spiritual philosophies such as Hinduism, Buddhism, Taoism, in the Hellenic 'Mystery-Religions', in the Hebrew and Jewish Old Testament and Christian New Testament of the Bible, in Eastern Christianity and Western Catholicism and Protestantism, in Islamic Sufism.

In the East, particularly India, it has been woven into the very fabric of history, inseparable from thousands of years of a tradition of 'seeking enlightenment' by means of those who have become enlightened. Mystic experience for the individual is not recorded as an event. Millions attempt it as a way of life: only the great originators of each Teaching make chronological history and they date from pre-history, with a few appearing in the recent past, but mostly as the inheritors, sometimes reincarnated, of the original Master.

European mystic history is quite different: it has what Evelyn Underhill, in her classic work *Mysticism*, calls 'a chronological curve'. Tracing it from the beginning of the Christian era to William Blake in the late 18th and early 19th centuries, she found that 'the great periods of mystical activity tend to correspond with the great periods of artistic, material, and intellectual civilisation', and come 'immediately after, and seem to complete such periods.'

To illustrate this point, in the Appendix of her book, Evelyn Underhill has provided a complete 'Historical Sketch', which gives the names and periods of every mystic who achieved recognition over the centuries, and it is soon apparent that they seemed to flourish in certain periods, to diminish in others.

Elmer O'Brien, a Jesuit scholar who wrote *Varieties of Mystic Experience* says the explanation of this is '. . . not that a time and place favorable to mysticism brings mystics into existence. Rather would it seem to be that a time and place favorable to mysticism bring into existence the recording of their experiences by which, alone, we have knowledge that the mystics existed. Other times, other places, likely have had mystics in much the same quantity; there is no reason for thinking they did not. Mysticism, however, was not in favor. So a literary silence cloaks them, wholly.'

Whatever the reason, in the West, mystics and saints seemed to reach a numerical peak in the Middle Ages in Church-dominated societies, then thinned-out towards the end of the 17th century and dwindled to an exceptional few, when they appeared to have succumbed almost altogether under the questioning scrutiny of psychology and science in the 19th century.

Looked at in this approximate sequence, the impression is that the saints and mystics of the Western world were a phenomenon, or product, of times gone by. Although their teachings remained to inspire and influence, such mystic fervour, such intense relationship with an invisible presence that it led to complete self-annihilation, torturous asceticism, and in some cases death for 'heresy', had vanished or at least gone underground.

Further than this, the reputations of the outstanding religious mystics of the past – Plotinus, St Augustine, Jan Van Ruysbroek, St Teresa of Avila, St John of the Cross among them – were no longer even sacrosanct. Psychoanalysis dissected the 'holy' aspect of mystic experience and found it fitted the category of fanaticism. No saint was exempt from having illustrated a form of mental illness ranging from mild to extreme.

The effect of this was to close the mouths of those whose opinion differed; claims to mystic experience were rare enough to confirm that they belonged to an obsolete past. Who would dare to say otherwise and be considered 'odd', admit not only to instability but the symptoms of neurosis?

That Eastern mystic experience lingered on was not much help to the prevailing Western view – which was, roughly, that in India people died in the streets, many mystics opting out from all concern by turning off their sensibilities and escaping into 'Cosmic Bliss', very conveniently shrinking their stomachs and thereby their desire for food, or wandering about with a begging bowl for scraps, conferring spiritual 'merits' on the donors. Altogether, towards the end of the 19th century the Western view of mystic experience was a grey and questionable area of modern civilisation.

In this bleak perspective, one beacon was lit in defence of mysticism when support came from a totally unexpected quarter, the world of medicine. In 1872 Richard Maurice Bucke, a Canadian doctor and psychologist, while on a visit to England underwent a mystical experience so profound that it was to become the centre of his outlook on life. He records: 'I had spent the evening in a great city, with two friends, reading and discussing poetry and philosophy. We parted at midnight. I had a long drive in a hansom to my lodging. My mind, deeply under the influence of the ideas, images and emotions called up by reading and talk, was calm and peaceful. I was in a state of quiet, almost passive enjoyment, not actually thinking, but letting ideas, images, and emotions flow of themselves, as it were, through my mind. All at once, without warning of any kind, I found myself wrapped in a flame-colored cloud. For an instant I thought of fire, an immense conflagration somewhere close by in that great city; the next, I knew that the fire was within myself. Directly afterward there came upon me a sense of exultation, of immense joyousness accompanied or immediately followed by an intellectual illumination impossible to believe, but I saw that the universe is not composed of dead matter, but is on the contrary, a living Presence; I became conscious in myself of eternal life. It was not a conviction that I would have eternal life, but a consciousness that I possessed eternal life then; I saw that all men are immortal; that the cosmic order is such that without any peradventure all things work together for the good of each and all; that the foundation principle of the world, of all the worlds, is what we call love, and that the happiness of each and all is in the long run absolutely certain. The vision lasted a few seconds and was gone but the memory of it and the sense of the reality of what it taught have remained during the quarter of a century which has since elapsed. I had attained to a point of view from which I saw that it must be true. That view, that conviction, I may say that consciousness, has never, even during periods of the deepest depression, been lost.'

Richard Bucke was 36 at the time, and this experience was to become the pivot of his mental energies. His first paper on the subject, which he entitled 'Cosmic Consciousness' was given before the American-Medico-Psychological Association in Philadelphia and another, given for his presidential address to the British Medical Association in Montreal, dealt with this theme. Four years later, he wrote *Cosmic Consciousness* (1901), a book which was to be the first of its kind and world-famous as a definitive study of mystic experience from the standpoint of *psychology*.

His detailed interpretation of mystic experience and of those who had had the experience was exhaustively developed from close study of the last 3000 years of history. Taking 50 instances for illustration, starting with Gautama the Buddha, Jesus the Christ and Paul, he advanced through many great and famous names of religious leaders, poets and writers, to end with more recent accounts that were identified only by initials.

Of these 50, Dr Bucke considered that there had been at least 14 cases that were undeniable experiences of complete and permanent 'Illumination', but many others that were partial or temporary. He also pointed out that some of the most renowned authorities on the subject of mystic experience left no proof that they had ever actually had the experience itself: he spoke of Plotinus as wanting desperately to have it, to the extent that he could convey it just as well as if he had, so that it was never questioned that he was a mystic.

Dr Bucke also noted what he saw as an increasing frequency of the experience, from which he concluded that mankind is in the gradual process of developing a more advanced form of consciousness that will eventually lift it out of all its present imperfections.

In the final analysis, however, his survey not only leaves mystics as set apart and of special predisposition, but sets limits as to the age and sex when it is most likely they will have their experience of cosmic consciousness: the preponderance of mystics, he said, would be men, and the experience would occur mostly while they were in their thirties.

These potential candidates, he concluded, appeared at intervals in human history, showing 'the first faint beginnings of another race; walking the earth and breathing the air with us, but at the same time walking another earth and breathing another air of which we know little or nothing, but which is, all the same, our spiritual life, as its absence would be our spiritual death . . .

While *Cosmic Consciousness* remains a pioneer work of enormous value as a study, books with a less restricted speculation have intervened, among them expanded anthologies of mystical experience from all walks of life, such as those of Raynor C. Johnson's referred to in the introduction to this book. These include, alongside the acclaimed mystics, numerous 'ordinary' people of this century, most of whom were still reluctant to be identified beyond their initials; some are experiences taken from works of fiction or fictionalised biography, which while conveying ecstatic beauty in the language of the mystic tend to keep the answers to overall significance at a remove.

Three descriptions of Bliss When one looks only at firsthand accounts of mystical experience, such as those which are the substance of this exploration, they assume a historical perspective. Consider, for instance, these three sincere and struggling efforts to describe the immediacy of the event – one from the Middle Ages, in the nature of a revelation of God, one from the recent past, expressing a sense of loving unity with all humanity, and one from the present, in which the experience took the form of perceiving the very essence of the natural world and identifying with it.

The first is that of Angela of Foligno (1248-1309) who left a very worldly life to become a tertiary hermit of the Franciscan Order.

'The eyes of my soul were opened and I discerned the fullness of God, in which I understood the whole world, here and beyond the sea, the abyss, the ocean, everything. In all these things I could see nothing except the divine power, in a way that was utterly indescribable. My soul was brimming over with wonder and cried out in a loud voice "The whole world is full of God" . . .'

And in another excerpt:

'I beheld a Thing, as fixed and stable as it was indescribable, and more than this I cannot say, save what I have often said already, namely that it was all good. And though my soul did not behold love, yet when it saw that ineffable Thing it was itself filled with unutterable joy, and was taken out of the state it was in and placed in this great and ineffable state . . . But if you want to know what it was that I beheld, I can tell you nothing, except that I beheld a Fullness and a Clearness, and felt them within me so abundantly that I cannot describe it, nor offer any image of it; for what I beheld was not bodily, but as though it were in heaven. Thus I beheld a beauty so great that I can say nothing of it except that I saw Supreme Beauty, which contains in itself all goodness.'

This second experience happened to the Indian poet Rabindranath Tagore (1861-1941), while he was standing watching the sun rise above the trees in a street in Calcutta. He told it to his friend C.F. Andrews, who recorded in his collection of letters:

'As I was watching it, suddenly, in a moment, a veil seemed to be lifted from my eyes. I found the world wrapped in an inexpressible glory with its waves of joy and beauty bursting and breaking on all sides. The thick cloud of sorrow that lay on my heart in many folds was pierced through and through by the light of the world, which was everywhere radiant . . .

'There was nothing and no one whom I did not love at that moment . . . I stood on the veranda and watched the coolies as they tramped down the road. Their movement, their forms, their countenances seemed strangely wonderful to me, as if they were all moving like waves in the great ocean of the world. When one young man placed his hand upon the shoulder of another and passed laughingly by, it was a remarkable event to me . . . I seemed to witness, in the wholeness of my vision, the movements of the body of all humanity, and to feel the beat of the music and the rhythm of a mystic dance.'

The third experience is contemporary and occurred to Derek Gibson, who describes himself as a serious, self-searching type, when he was forty-six. He was working for a firm on the outskirts of Portsmouth and used to travel to work by motorcycle, making an early start. One morning in 1969 he was following his usual route when he had his first encounter with the transcendent:

'The road was absolutely clear of traffic and people. I had slowed my speed to take a corner when I noticed first that the sound of my motorcycle engine faded to a murmur. I thought something was wrong and glanced down. The rhythm of the engine was normal though so I looked up again. I thought how beautiful the morning was (even though everything was in semi-darkness).

'Then everything suddenly changed. I could clearly see everything as before with form and substance, but instead of looking AT it all I was looking INTO everything. I saw beneath the bark of the trees and *through* the underlying trunks. I was looking *into* the grass too, and all was magnified beyond measure. To the extent that I could see moving microscopic organisms! Then, not only was I seeing all this, but I was literally *inside* it all. *At the same time* as I was looking into this mass of greenery I was aware of every single blade of grass and fold of the trees as if each had been placed before me one at a time and entered into.

'My world became a fairyland of vivid greens and browns, colours

not seen so much as felt. Instantly also my mind was not observ̶̶
but was living what it was registering. "I" did not exist. Power and
knowledge surged through my mind. The words formed in me. I can
remember clearly "Now *I* know", "There is *nothing I* could not answer.
I am a part of all this". I looked up to the sky to behold the most
wonderful view of starlight I have ever seen. The heavens were filled
with absolutely brilliant stars, larger than is usual and so close that but
for the grasses and trees before me I would have been among them.
Once again those words formed. "*You* know, *you* know".

'Now began a second wonder. *An absolute sense of peace and joy
overtook me.* I lost all sense of being "me". I had identity but it was not
me as I regard myself. I was out there a part of all that was before me,
and I was not alone. There was a 'presence' not seen but my senses were
aware of it.

'Then I noticed that all this sensation was withdrawing from me
slowly. The note of my motorcycle engine intruded more until I felt
myself once again almost normal yet slightly lightheaded.

'The sensation of what had happened lingered all day. I filled my
thoughts with it trying to recapture it. For weeks I wondered at it, not
trying to fathom it but just to enjoy it all. On one or two occasions
during that period I did manage to recover the feeling of peace, but
weakly.

'These "peace and joy" experiences can happen at anytime and anywhere,
but are usually outdoors. There is that glorious feeling of being lifted
out of myself and becoming part of everything around me. I do not
have any visions or further X-ray ability as in 1969. My mind is suddenly
filled with peace and happiness and then it loses its singularity. I am just
not "me" anymore. I am part of the very air around me. I feel "up there"
in the sky. "Outside looking in – and inside looking out". How can
words convey such things? I can only describe them as best I am able.'

From these experiences of the mystic taken from different times and
cultures, the differences tend only to underscore the similarities. Are
mystics still to be considered as having very rare and special qualities?
Is mystic experience dying out along with the charismatic element of
religion – or on the increase? Or – has it always been prevalent, muted
by a conspiracy of discomfort, fear of ridicule for being vulnerable to
such uncontrolled flights from the normal and real?

A few years ago, the idea of research into the subject as it pertains to
the present day began to surface here and there in the form of surveys.
Perhaps some missing explanations can be found within their statistical
enquiries, several of which now follow.

2
Bliss Research

Contemporary Research and Surveys

'. . . the national sample may be the only way to begin the
study of mystical experience in modern society' — Andrew
M. Greeley and William C. McCready (*New York Times
Magazine*, 1975)

For many years following Richard Bucke's pioneer work, research took
a long, devious route through and around the subject of mystic experience.
As science closed in it was safer to relate such vague and suspect studies
to the psychology of religion, to inquire why people went to church or
stayed away, believed or did not believe in God, why they needed God
or belief at all. There was an underlying implied bias toward Freudian
views and against the normality of those who communed with 'the
Divine'.

The climate of the 1960s, with its loosening of conventional rigidities,
was more favourable. Mystic experience sidled back into focus under
the cover of a barely more respectable search into the subject of
'consciousness'. The availability of 'mind-changing' drugs and the
popularisation of meditation in the West by gurus from the East, led to
widespread interest in 'inner space'. In such a setting the evidence of a
possible spiritual content to life — one that could be legitimately included
in the realm of scales, tests, polls and surveys — became admissible.

The term 'mystic experience' was still avoided. 'Ecstasy' or 'transcendent
experience' were those used by Marghanita Laski in her well-received
book, *Ecstasy: A Study of Some Secular and Religious Experiences*
(1961). 'Peak' experience was the term used by Abraham Maslow in his
Religions, Values, and Peak Experiences (1964) to describe what he
called the 'self-actualising process' of which he became the pioneer in
America; he observed that the 'peak' experiences 'have been highly
therapeutic for some people, and for others a whole outlook on life
has been changed forever by some great moment of insight or inspiration

or conversion'.

Along with 'consciousness' research and these and other psychological approaches that still tended to be gathered under the umbrella of Religion, came a growing speculative interest in the statistical element of religious experience as applied to these intense, individual 'flashes of illumination'. How *many* people had them in a sampling of the population? What were they like? How long did they last? With what frequency did they occur? At what age? What was their subsequent or ultimate effect?

In 1969, Sir Alister Hardy (mentioned on page 4) decided it was time to make a systematic exploration. With the establishment of his Religious Experience Research Unit (RERU) at Manchester College, Oxford, a large-scale survey of a non-scientific, purely subjective pheno-menon was launched with the method and objectivity of science.

Sir Alister's goal was to collect 5,000 samples of ordinary people's spontaneous religious experiences (rather than those induced by some consciousness-altering means), offering them complete anonymity. All they had to do was write down what they had experienced and send it in to RERU. Making his request known through religious publications, Sir Alister was at first disappointed with the mere 250 replies, but later he was interviewed by several leading newspapers and wrote articles about his research and the replies became more plentiful.

The experiences gradually accumulated and were collated, categorised and carefully studied. Sir Alister was assisted by a number of qualified academics with a special interest in the ramifications of such a study. Several of these later did their own extended research in associated areas – much of which is contained in Sir Alister's book *The Spiritual Nature of Man* (1979).

The first 1,000 samples proved disappointing. There was much overlapping of contents that raised more questions than it answered and introduced a disconcerting complexity of classification. In such a personal and sensitive matter Sir Alister had not wanted to approach people with a form to fill in, but now, in the second stage of the research, he conceded that it might be necessary.

A questionnaire was developed by him and his staff and sent to selected people who had already sent in their religious experience. Their response brought some helpful if limited clarification of category.

The Spiritual Nature of Man gives an account of the first eight years' work of the Unit, Sir Alister sets out the 12 main divisions and sub-divisions of the various elements found in the first 3,000 de-scriptions of intense religious experience; these were examined in his own words, 'as a contribution towards the study of this important, but still so little understood, part of our make-up made in the spirit of an inquiring naturalist' the figures given against each category explain the average occurrence per thousand of that particular element in the over-all 3,000 records:

1. **Sensory or quasi-sensory experience: visual**
   - (a) Visions (181.3)
   - (b) Illuminations (45)
   - (c) A particular light (88)
   - (d) Feeling of unity with surroundings and/or with other people (59.3)
   - (e) 'Out-of-the-body' (59.7)
   - (f) 'Déjà vu (5.3)
   - (g) Transformation of surroundings (24.3)
2. **Sensory or quasi-experience: auditory**
   - (a) 'Voices', calming (73.7)
   - (b) 'Voices', guiding (70)
   - (c) 'Being spoken through', gift of tongues (31)
   - (d) 'Music' and other sounds (23)
3. **Sensory or quasi-sensory experience: touch**
   - (a) Healing (15.3)
   - (b) Comforting (29)
   - (c) Feelings of warmth, etc. (53.7)
   - (d) Being hit, shocked, etc. (18.3)
   - (e) Guiding (5.3)
4. **Sensory or quasi-sensory experience: smell**
5. **Supposed extra-sensory perception**
   - (a) Telepathy (36.7)
   - (b) Precognition (69.3)
   - (c) Clairvoyance (15.3)
   - (d) Supposed contact with the dead (79.7)
   - (e) Apparitions (34)
6. **Behavioural changes: enhanced or 'superhuman' power displayed by man**
   - (a) Comforting, guiding (27)
   - (b) Healing (34.3)
   - (c) Exorcism (3.7)
   - (d) Heroism (6.3)
7. **Cognitive and affective elements**
   - (a) Sense of security, protection, peace (253)
   - (b) Sense of joy, happiness, well-being (212)

(c) Sense of new strength in oneself (65)

(d) Sense of guidance, vocation, inspiration (157.7)

(e) Awe, reverence, wonder (66)

(f) Sense of certainty, clarity, enlightenment (194.7)

(g) Exaltation, excitement, ecstasy (47.3)

(h) Sense of being at a loss for words (25.3)

(i) Sense of harmony, order, unity (66.7)

(j) Sense of timelessness (37.7)

(k) Feeling of love, affection (in oneself) (56.7)

(l) Yearning, desire, nostalgia (14.3)

(m) Sense of forgiveness, restoration, renewal (40)

(n) Sense of integration, wholeness, fulfilment (12.7)

(o) Hope, optimism (15.3)

(p) Sense of release from fear of death (36.3)

(q) Fear, horror (41.7)

(r) Remorse, sense of guilt (23.7)

(s) Sense of indifference, detachment (11.3)

(t) Sense of purpose behind events (113.7)

(u) Sense of prayer answered in events (138.3)

(v) Sense of presence (not human) (202.3)

8. Development of experience

(i) Within the individual

(a) Steady disposition; little or no development recorded (1.3)

(b) Gradual growth of sense of awareness: experience more or less continuous (91.3)

(c) Sudden change to a new sense of awareness, conversion, the 'moment of truth' (175.3)

(d) Particular experiences, no growth recorded (13.7)

(e) Particular experiences, each contributing to growth of sense of awareness (145.7)

(ii) In relation to others

(k) Identification with ideal human figure, discipleship, hero-worship (6)

(l) Development by personal encounter (113)

(m) Participation in church, institutional, or corporate life (29.7)

(n) Development through contact with literature or the arts (117.7)

(o) Experience essentially individualistic, involving isolation from or rejection by others (27)

(iii) Periods of significant development

(r) In childhood (117.7)

(s) In adolescence (123.7)

(t) In middle age (70.3)
(u) In old age (7.7)

9. Dynamic patterns in experience

(i) Positive or constructive
  (a) Initiative felt to be beyond the self, coming 'out of the blue', grace (124)
  (b) Initiative felt to lie within the self, but response from beyond; prayers answered (322.7)
  (c) Initiative and response both felt as within the self; the result seen as 'individuation' (Jung), 'self-actualization' (Maslow) (4.7)
  (d) Differentiation between initiative and response felt as illusory; merging of the self into the All; the unitive experience (22.3)
(ii) Negative or destructive
  (m) Sense of external evil force as having initiative (44.7)

10. Dream experiences (87.7)

11. Antecedents or 'triggers' of experience

(i) (a) Natural beauty (122.7)
   (b) Sacred places (26)
   (c) Participation in religious worship (117.7)
   (d) Prayer, meditation (135.7)
   (e) Music (56.7)
   (f) Visual art (24.7)
   (g) Literature, drama, film (82)
   (h) Creative work (20.7)
   (i) Physical activity (9.7)
   (j) Relaxation (16.7)
   (k) Sexual relations (4)
   (l) Happiness (7.3)
   (m) Depression, despair (183.7)
   (n) Illness (80)
   (o) Childbirth (8.7)
   (p) The prospect of death (15.3)
   (q) The death of others (28)
   (r) Crises in personal relations (37.3)
   (s) Silence, solitude (15.3)
(ii) (w) Drugs: anaesthetic (10.7)
   (x) Drugs: psychedelic (6.7)

12. Consequences of experience

   (a) Sense of purpose or new meaning to life (184.7)
   (b) Changes in religious belief (38.7)
   (c) Changes in attitude to others (77)

Sir Alister goes on to explain and illustrate in detail the fine and subtle points of this wide variety of interior experience, much of which is to some extent pertinent to a contemporary exploration. For this purpose, it can be seen that the main divisions and sub-divisions to be considered here, in our study of the Bliss experience and its related components are to be found among those of 7. *'Cognitive and affective elements'.*

While there is overlap even in this distinctive category, it is never in basic self-contradiction; the experience is not only overwhelmingly rapturous, unmistakably enlightening, but it stands aside from any confinement of time, place, person or thing. According to Sir Alister, without giving his examples of experience with which this book will abound, these 'cognitive' moments of joy occur in 636 accounts out of the 3000: 'just over 21 per cent of the records sent in.'

From this remarkable attempt at statistical classification, which Sir Alister feels is only a beginning, quantitative research has proceeded in various branches off the main stem, the questionnaires expanding this or that significance of religious experience in an ever-increasing approach to the deepest roots of the tree itself.

In America in 1974 two researchers, Andrew Greeley and William McCready of the National Opinion Research Center at the University of Chicago, came up with very different findings from those of Richard Bucke some 70 years earlier. Whereas Bucke had traced only 50 people throughout all history who had ever experienced 'cosmic consciousness', Andrew Greeley and William McCready discovered from a national poll of 1,500 persons, that about 600 reported having had at least one mystic experience, about 300 of them several times, and 75 of them often; in other words, more than three out of every ten Americans (35%)!

This was quite a surprise to the researchers, themselves 'thoroughly unmystical', and motivated purely by curiosity, who had managed to find room for a few questions on mystic experience in a representative national survey of 'ultimate values' among 1500 American adults. They merely wanted to know how many people in American society had had such experience, and what kind of effect the experience had had on them. They settled on the question: 'Have you ever had the feeling of being very close to a powerful spiritual force that seemed to lift you out of yourself?' yes.

Lacking the time or finance to extend their request for more details of each experience, the researchers presented the respondents with two lists of questions to be answered. One list suggested possible ways in which the experience had been 'triggered' ('the trigger-factor' was a term coined by Marghanita Laski in her book *Ecstasy* to describe the condition or feeling which seemed to set the experience in motion). The other list contained suggestions of what the experience had been like.

The answers indicated that the questions had been the right ones: 'A feeling that I couldn't possibly describe was happening to me'; 'the sensation that my personality had been taken over by something much more powerful than I am'; 'a sense that I was being bathed in light'; 'a sense of a new life or living in a new world', came together in a pattern so distinct that the researchers called it the 'twice-born factor'.

Without means of proving with certainty that this substantial segment of the American population were all 'mystics', there was suspension of judgement and further analysis of the responses:

'Who are the ones who have mystical experiences?' they asked. The answer was that people in their 40s and 50s were somewhat more likely to report them than those younger or older. Protestants were more likely than Jews, and Jews more likely than Catholics (further breakdown of this category indicated that the Episcopalians within the Protestant denominations were more frequent mystics than the fundamentalists). Lastly the Irish, Protestant or Catholic, were more likely than any of these to be 'mystics'.

'Who are those who have these episodes often?' It would seem that they are 'disproportionately' male, black, college-educated, above the $10,000-a-year income level and Protestant.

The respondents were also not the socially or economically disadvantaged, and even of the blacks not among the poor but the college-educated. Nor were their backgrounds in general unhappy; they came from families with a close relationship and some affiliation with religion. Although there was no opportunity to administer complex personality tests or in-depth interviews, the researchers did use the *Psychological Well-Being Scale* developed by Professor Norman Bradburn (of the National Opinion Research Center). The resultant .40 was the highest correlation between frequent ecstatic states and psychological well-being that Professor Bradburn had ever observed with his scale.

After more random interviews with other researchers, students and colleagues who now came out into the open to report their own mystic experiences, Andrew Greeley and William McCready came to certain conclusions. There were far more mystics about than had ever been supposed; this fact should be more extensively investigated. Other than this, they had nothing but speculation to offer (their views will be added in the Summary of this Chapter).

A few years later (1978), further quantitative research into religious experience was again conducted in Britain. David Hay, a zoologist with a longstanding interest in religion as a biological and cultural phenomenon and associated with Sir Alister Hardy's RERU, carried out two national surveys in co-operation with Ann Morisy, a sociologist.

One was founded on questions taken from a standard nation-wide survey done by National Opinion Polls Ltd., in which 1865 people (853 male and 1012 female) were asked to respond to questions on religious experience. The other was based on a more personal in-depth line of questioning, by means of discreet interviews of a randomly-selected number of people in and around Nottingham. These complementary pieces of research, which have been considerably publicised and broadcast on television in the U.K., emerged with a percentage similar to Andrew Greeley and William McCready's: 36% of the British population had had one or more experiences of a mystic nature.

In his book, *Exploring Inner Space* (1982), David Hay has since delved into the many aspects of this study, but arrives at the same conclusions as the American researchers, restraining his own interpretations and bias for the objective evidence that more people have mystic experience than has so far been apparent and that much more detailed investigation is needed:

'I doubt very much that religion is about to die out,' he says. 'The awareness out of which it grows is too widespread for that. More dangerous, because more likely, is that it may continue to be isolated from the mainstream of modern life. Human realities which are absolutely ignored tend, as Freud has pointed out, to return in bizarre and fanatical forms . . . . We need to attend more openly to our religious awareness, so that at the very least its constructiveness and creativity can be used for the benefit of the species.'

The Report by the Group for the Advancement of Psychiatry

'Experience may be judged as invalidly mad or as validly mystical. The distinction is not easy' – R.D. Laing, *The Politics of Consciousness*

In this century, psychoanalysis first, then psychiatry, gradually reduced mankind's mind-body relationship to an inter-play of the unconscious-subconscious-conscious aspects of his being. Everything that did not conform to the rational, perceivable, 'normal' reality could be labelled,

classified, categorised as degrees of mental imbalance ranging from
mild neurosis to psychotic disorder. The cause was traced back to
childhood and the cure sought by leading the disturbed patient to re-
live, dream-out, empty-out the offending traumatic events, whereupon
he would adjust, adapt, relate more happily, more efficiently to the
world-as-it-is in 'reality'.

Mystic experience fell almost completely under this hammer, became
the most suspect of all symptoms, so that even those who might have
experienced it firsthand, with no other apparent signs of instability,
suspected themselves. More often than not they would tell nobody in
case it was true that they were hallucinating, hysterical, escaping from
adulthood, regressing to the womb, or betraying signs of any one of a
number of dire mental illnesses. After all, were not even the saints of old
now diagnosed as paranoiacs, schizophrenics or manic-depressives and
most mystics as suffering from one form or another of masochism or
religious mania? Even *mysticism* itself was rolled up and filed away
under the heading of '*scientific ignorance*'.

Understandable as it may have been through the early part, and even
middle, of the century, it was remarkable in the '70s that a committee of
psychiatrists should make an investigation of the phenomena of mystic
experience and reach exactly the same conclusions.

In their report, *Mysticism: Spiritual Quest or Psychic Disorder* (U.S.,
1976), the Group for the Advancement of Psychiatry first aspired to
define the subtle dividing line between mystic experience and mental
derangement, presenting non-psychiatric definitions of mysticism and
characteristics of mystic experience, distinguishing and describing its
various categories, stages and phases from its broadest aspects through
to 'the more or less typical course that has been called "the Mystic Way"
(Evelyn Underhill's term), which leads to religious conversion'.

The report also described the different interpretations mystics put on
their awesome experience, the fact that some see 'the supernatural' as
personal, and speak of a 'spiritual marriage between God and the soul'
(St Teresa of Jesus), while some see it as a call to emerge from the role of
recluse to religious leader with a duty to save the world. It then mentioned
that Jewish mystics indicate a 'clinging to God', rather than a merging
with Him, and summarized its abstract of mysticism with a brief reference
to mysticism of the East, which 'insists on still another step along the
mystical path: total annihilation of the self and its absorption into the
Infinite, as expressed in the Sufis' Eighth Stage of Progress and Buddhists'
Nirvana.'

An attempt to analyse the Group's problems in drawing up the Report, made still more difficult by the different viewpoints of its members, was put as follows:

'The inability of this Committee to make a firm distinction between a mystical state and a psychopathological state may be due, in part at least, to more fundamental theoretical problems in psychiatry. The many ways in which human behaviour and thought can be perceived make numerous points of view inevitable. For example, there are those who draw fine lines between various psychiatric diagnoses as irrelevant and who perceive in schizophrenia a manifestation to be prized as a way toward better adaption. Pathology may be uncovered in the nature of – and the method of resolution of – the conflicts in someone who seems to be brimming over with mental health, while the thought and behavior of the most disturbed patient may be viewed as a contribution to his well-being. Therefore we should not expect to be able to reach a consensus on the line distinguishing mysticism from mental disorder. From one point of view all mystical experiences may be regarded as symptoms of mental disturbance, and from another, they may be regarded as attempts at adaptation.

'. . .we might have gone further', the Report conceded, 'with our psychoanalytic interpretation had caution or disagreement not stopped us. For one thing, we might have expanded our discussion on the nature of the childhood events that contribute to adult proclivities toward mysticism. To cite one example, we could have theorized about a connection between the development of awe in childhood and mystical states in adulthood. Saint Catherine of Siena was a mystic who reported having highly developed feelings of awe at the age of five, when she saw the Lord "in the most sacred and awe-inspiring garb imaginable" above the Sienese church of San Domenico.' Phyllis Greenacre in *The Psychoanalytic Study of the Child* (1956) suggested that childhood feelings of awe and religious feeling are often derived from awe (as distinguished from envy) of the phallus. In the girl, awe is more liable to be aroused, if the child sees an adult phallus rather than a boy's.'

The similarities between the workings of the creative processes and those of mystical experience were another theme incorporated in the Report. Concerning the analytic psychology of C.G. Jung, in its closer association with the mystic element of man through his concept of *archetypes* and a *collective unconscious*, GAP referred to a discussion of Jungian mysticism by Erich Neumann (in *The Mystic Vision: Papers from the Eranos Yearbooks*, 1968). According to this writer, C.G. Jung's view of man is that he is a '*Homo mysticus*', and that mystical phenomena contribute to personality development, all of which are essential to all creative processes. 'Mystical experiences are not only theistic, extroverted and introverted, 'but give rise to love, artistic creation, great ideas and delusions.'

While agreeing with Sigmund Freud that 'projection' plays a part in mystic experience, Erich Neumann believed that many analysts, by failing to recognise the 'vital significance of archetypes and the collective unconscious' arrived at interpretations that were 'reductionist and personalistic' . . . 'For mysticism is inherent in man, and every mystical experience (or, in Jungian terms, every encounter between the ego and the numinous) transforms his personality and what is more – "the development of (man's) natural phases with their archetypal encounters gives a mystical stamp to the development of every man, even though he may be unaware of it"'.

From its standpoint that mystic experience is ultimately psychiatrically explicable, the GAP report saw its chief value as a *study*:

'The psychiatrist will find mystical phenomena of interest because they can demonstrate forms of behaviour intermediate between normality and frank psychosis; a form of ego regression in the service of defense against internal or external stress; and a paradox of the return of repressed regression in unconventional expressions of love.'

Among the 'Case Reports' most of them in the category best suited to psychiatric interpretation, with the sensory, visual phenomena stressed rather than the so-called 'higher states' of mysticism – the one quoted here provides an example of a typical conclusion. The woman cited was in psychotherapy and had had an experience similar to that of the great religious mystics: 'Her interests were reinvested in the fantasy universe, representing God, in which such problems do not exist, and she felt herself united with this God-Universe, a substitute for an unavailable or rejecting parent. The mystical union made up for the rejection she feared from her father, now represented by the therapist in another man . . .' The report did add, open-endedly, that the 'illusion of knowledge' that came to her stimulated her to seek further knowledge and led 'directly to the disappearance of her inhibition to serious reading 'and increased creativity'.

Finally, in sections discussing aspects of Christian and Hindu mysticism, the GAP reported with greater objectivity, and sat in judgement on, 'the naive Western observers of the Indian scene', saying:

'Confronted by such common symbols as that of the representation of the divine activity in sexual form, and bewildered by the profusion of deities in the Hindu pantheon, they could impute to Hinduism a "decadence" following from its essence, and they fail to apply to that religion the discrimination between enlightened and superstitious observance which they would be sure to demand for their own.'

While there appears to be a chink here and there in the psychiatric consensus, at least some concession being made to the possible therapeutic benefits of mystic experience, the impasse between psychiatry and mysticism largely remains.

A Summary of Statistical and Psychiatric Approaches

'The miracle is that the universe created a part of itself to study the rest of it . . .' – John C. Lilly, *Center of the Cyclone* (1961)

While the revelations of national polls and surveys on religious or intensely 'spiritual' experiences provide statistical evidence that 'mystics' and mystic experience are not the rare phenomena that was supposed, they appear to have opened the way to more questions rather than to established conclusions.

Sir Alister Hardy, at the end of his immensely detailed inquiry wrote: 'Perhaps to the point of tedium I have several times stressed the importance of making more studies of the many different aspects of our growing collections of material; if the foregoing points do in fact represent the main characteristics of man's spiritual life on the religious side, they need to be filled out in all kinds of ways and extended in many directions. The studies must be applied to other cultures, other faiths. . . . It is vital, I believe, that we should establish whether these characteristics which we have been discussing are indeed applicable to mankind as a whole.'

Sir Alister also speaks of the possible debate on the significance of these elements for man's philosophy of life, for they 'tend to undermine some cherished modern dogmas' . . . [nevertheless] . . . 'many more changes will come in our scientific outlook. Man has had so many of his illusions shattered and swept away over the centuries that I doubt if a change in our concept of the nature and the location of God will be more shocking than finding that the earth was round and not at the centre of the universe, or that man was not separately created. We are due for another change. The spiritual nature of man is, I believe, being shown to be a reality. We now need a new biological philosophy which will recognize both this and the need to study consciousness as a fundamental attribute of life. . . . How much faster would be the progress if only a tithe of the resources devoted to physical and chemical research would be available to provide so many more to take part in the exploration. I have the faith to believe that it will come before it is too late.'

Despite their substantial evidence that more than three out of every ten Americans (35%) had had an intense spiritual experience, perhaps of a mystical nature, the National Opinion Poll Researchers, Andrew Greeley and William McCready still wonder whether such a question ('Have you ever had the feeling of being very close to a powerful spiritual force that seemed to lift you out of yourself?') could really 'get at' the true classic meaning of the word 'mystical' experience.

'Until further research is done,' they wrote, 'we cannot say for sure. Obviously, one has to know far more about the experience that an individual respondent has had than can be gleaned in a first-round exploration. No survey question is ever perfect and doubtless this one is in many respects inadequate. If there is more research on mysticism, whoever does it will probably find better ways to ask the question . . .

'On the other hand, someone has to ask the question for the first time or there will be nothing on which to improve. But we are moderately hopeful that the wording of the question is accurate enough for our present exploratory purposes.' If the more than two-thirds of those who have had experiences suggested by the question which placed them at the top end of a seven-point intensity scale, did not have the classic 'mystical' experience, 'it is nonetheless a striking phenomenon that a large segment of the population is prepared to report such an intense experience. Whatever the nature of that experience, and however much it might fit the definition of traditional mysticism, it is in itself worth investigating . . .

'Finally, is the world as joyous and as benign, as loving and dazzling a place as the "mystics" – those in the classic literature as well as in our samples – claim it is?

'Well,' the poll-report concludes, 'as sociologists, we can't say for sure. But it would be nice if it were.'

The surveys of David Hay and Ann Morisy, having investigated more intimate and detailed accounts of spiritual experience, revealed many surprises for the researchers. These were mainly to do with the variety of the experiences, their prevalence, and the willingness of the respondents to answer openly and as best they could the 'key questions' they were asked.

In reports published in 1978 and 1979 in the *Journal for the Scientific Study of Religion*, the researchers set out the results of their British polls in a set of Tables showing the percentage of responses in these categories:

overall frequency (of the experience); response compared with terminal education age; response compared with age; with social class; with psychological well-being; geographical distribution; denominations; church attendance; importance of the spiritual experience; time it lasted; alone, or in the company of other people; state of mind before it happened; state of mind after it was over; whether experience was religious; effect on outlook on life.

Although many of the experiences related could only broadly be classified as 'mystic', some of the generalised conclusions proved to be of interest for further research:

In the category of frequency, for instance, while it is a 'common experience', it is not at all common in occurrence, happening preponderantly only once or twice (spontaneously) in a lifetime; older people were more likely to have spiritual experiences than the young; the more educated, the more likely to at least claim to have had such experience; more middle class and upper class people have religious experience compared to the unskilled labourers, skilled working class and lower-middle class (which tallies with American studies); in both American and British studies, the most frequent reports come from areas where people regularly attend church – Wales, Scotland and the South-West in the U.K., the Southern States in the U.S. The lowest reports come from large cities, the highest from small towns; a blurred area, where varying forms of Christian belief predominate, with Jews following and agnostics, atheists and those who 'don't know' trailing in frequency of experiences, but closely linked to the church-attendance category; yet only 56% of churchgoers altogether claim to have had a distinct spiritual experience, the rest adamant that they have *not*; the importance rates a 'very' from 74%; the experience for over half of the respondents lasted between a few seconds and ten minutes, though some last up to a day, a few up to a month, a year or longer; distress or uneasiness sometimes precedes these experiences (in their inclusive range); most people were completely alone when they had their experiences; state of mind afterwards was in the majority of reports peaceful, restored to well-being, elated, happy, uplifted, awestruck, though a small number were the opposite, exhausted or numbed; the essence of the experience was religious, associated with God; about three-quarters of the respondents felt it had changed their lives considerably.

In *Exploring Inner Space*, David Hay enlarged upon the significance of these various responses as they applied to religious attitudes and experience in Britain, and summarised the findings in these words: 'On the face of it we are presented here with an extraordinary phenomenon.

Why *should* so many people have religious experience to report?' If, based on the prediction of the surveys about fifteen million adults in the country would also say they had been 'aware of or influenced by a presence or a power...the results of the poll probably underestimate the actual totals of those who believe they have had this kind of experience.'

Despite the fact that his book, 'like other books, is liberally sprinkled with unsupported philosophical assumptions'...there is, he writes, 'one assumption that I do *not* make...that somehow or other these experiences "prove" that there is a God, except perhaps to the satisfaction of the person to whom the experience happened. On the other hand, they, like any other human experiences, are data which ought not to be ignored in making coherent sense of one's world. If they do not use traditional religious language, most people are struck dumb when they try to describe the meaning of their experience. This is evidence of how destitute contemporary models of reality are when it comes to dealing with these deeper aspects of life, not that they do not exist.'

Speaking of the David Hay/Ann Morisy survey, Sir Alister Hardy rounded out the value of these sociological studies by adding: '...Such quantitative analyses must, however, go hand in hand with a continuing attempt to gain an ever deeper understanding of the essence of those remarkable elements in his (man's) nature which can never be the subject of scientific inquiry: they are akin to those of art, poetry, love and affection which can be studied only through a careful comparison of qualitative accounts of human experience.'

As far as the GAP report is concerned, a rebuttal came from one of their own psychiatrists, Arthur J. Deikman in the *Journal of Nervous and Mental Disease* (1977), who said that although some sections of the report showed commendable objectivity and scholarship, as a whole, 'the report displays extreme parochialism, a lack of discrimination, and naive arrogance in its approach to the subject.

'It is truly remarkable to have a group of psychiatrists issue a report in 1976 in which the only comment they make on the mystic perception of unity is that it represents a "reunion with parents"... Nowhere in the report do we find a discussion of the possibility that the perception of unity occurring in the higher forms of mysticism may be correct and that the ordinary perception of separateness and meaninglessness may be an illusion, as mystics claim. Clearly, mystic perception could be true whether or not a particular mystic might wish, in fantasy, to be reunited with his or her mother.'

In his attempt to understand the phenomenon of the GAP report itself, Arther J. Deikman was led to two main considerations – first that in order to have appreciation of mystic experience, the psychiatrists themselves needed to experience it and have some firsthand knowledge of what they were trying to discuss – after all, in its own profession, psychiatrists were 'unwavering' in their requirement 'that one must "know" through experience, not just description.' Who would understand 'transference', for instance, without experiencing it, or meditation and its results? 'Participation by scientists in these areas of mysticism would result in an understanding that is less exotic and less religious – and would help rid ourselves of the clap-trap associated with mysticism that constitutes a burden to scientist and mystic alike.'

Most importantly, in his view, the GAP report did not show any sign of humility. 'Perhaps medicine's long battle to free itself from religious control, from demonology and "divine authority", has left us [psychiatrists] with an automatic and costly reaction against anything that bears the outward signs of religion . . .' But the authors of the Report also 'selectively ignored the central issues of mysticism, and made traditional interpretations of the secondary phenomena. . . . .

'If our profession is to advance, we must recognize our defenses against ideas that would change our assumptions. Mysticism, studied seriously, challenges basic tenets of Western cultures: a) the primacy of reason and intellect; b) the separate, individual nature of man; c) the linear organization of time . . . .

' . . . by permitting our vision to be narrowed so as to exclude the unfamiliar, we betray our integrity as psychiatrists, showing no more capacity for freedom from prejudice than persons totally ignorant of psychodynamics – perhaps less . . . .'

All in all, it seems certain that the nature of mystic experience is still far from clear, even under the microscope of modern research. Yet what is equally certain is that a start has been made in an effort to come to grips with it as a phenomenon of human existence.

3
Bliss as Spontaneous Experience

'Interpretations of the experience, including those given by
the mystic himself, never have the same almost indubitable
authority as do his descriptions of the experience itself' –
W.T. Stace, *Mysticism and Philosophy* (1960)

Studying large quantities of contemporary firsthand accounts of the
Bliss experience reveals another distinguishable element. This is the
curiously natural way in which they fall into two distinct categories:
those which are 'spontaneous' and those which are 'induced'.

The spontaneous experience is one that simply *happens*, without
warning, to the 'deserving' or undeserving, to the believer or the agnostic
or the atheist alike, to the young or old, to the educated or uneducated
man or woman of any race, colour or walk of life, at any time, in any
part of the world.

The induced experience is one that is the result of effort, of application,
of sustained pursuit, of deliberate induction or seduction by means of a
vast number of methods and techniques, including the use of drugs, of
spiritual systems East or West.

There are times, of course, when the edges of distinction blur and
what occurs as unsought, may long have been unconsciously sought.
These make a third category, which here are further separated and
defined as pursued or unpursued. For instance, the person who has had
a long and deeply-felt desire to experience the mystic cannot be considered
as inducing the experience by definite efforts: the desire, fulfilled, is still
a spontaneous event. An expectation may have lain dormant, he or
she may perhaps have had hints of the possibility, a sense of its approach,
and even have felt the stir of minor inspirations and borderline ecstasies:
still, the big moment when it comes has to be listed as spontaneous.

Any kind of a mystic life, way, maintained application by no matter
what means, is to be considered as pursued, or 'induced'. In other

words, the one experience is a reward, the other a 'gift'.

In the spontaneous experience, there is no need to refer to any particular mystical system, no necessity to analyse the various stages by which it is reached or to argue the right or best way to the ultimate illumination. It could seem unfair to those who have given their very lives to struggling to the top of the spiritual ladder that just any person who may have made no effort whatever to be purged or purified, might swear, drink, steal, lie, fornicate, commit adultery and hold mean thoughts about his neighbour, can yet be borne off into this dazzling, 'holy' realm as blessed as any saint.

Whether or not a person who has a completely unexpected spontaneous experience can be called a mystic as a result, or would even want to be, is another question, to be considered later in the book. Nor is the concern here with the ultimate source of the spontaneous experience, although in this context it is worth recalling the comment of John Bowker in his Wilde Lecture on The Sense of God: ' . . . We should not overlook the possibility that the origin of the sense of God is, in fact, God'.

First-Hand Accounts of the Experience Itself

'An inner illumination may change the whole significance of the thing perceived' – Raynor C. Johnson, *The Imprisoned Splendour*

In the examples which follow, the experiences have been chosen because they are firsthand accounts of the *spontaneous* variety, and because the experiencers were not in any way 'professional' mystics but simply a cross-section of people in today's world. They are not chosen for their claim to fame though they may be well-known. Nor are they often quoted in famous works and anthologies, and cannot be classed in any one life-style or background. No one of them required anonymity. All individual comments are given mainly in the person's own words, although for reasons of space here and there these have been summarised.

Some of the experiences are long and intense, others very brief both in the experiencing and the telling, but all share the quality of at least apparent unexpectedness.

The first encounter is that of a highly educated, self-aware, successful professional woman who, far from having spiritual leanings, described herself as a 'radical humanist'. The initial, overwhelming experience that transformed her life took place out of doors and lasted only a few minutes; a second, also brief, happened while driving, to be followed by less intense states lasting in some cases for days at a time.

'Awakening from a long, deep sleep'

Wendy Rose-Neill was tending her garden in Buckinghamshire one autumn day when the experience occurred. Although a medical journalist and psychotherapist, and therefore well used to communicating, it was with the greatest difficulty that she recorded what happened:

'...I had always found gardening a relaxing activity and on this particular day I felt in a very contemplative frame of mind. I remember that I gradually became intensely aware of my surroundings – the sound of the birds singing, the rustling of leaves, the breeze on my skin and the scent of the grass and flowers.

'I had a sudden impulse to lie face down on the grass and as I did so, an energy seemed to flow through me as if I had become part of the earth underneath me. The boundary between my physical self and my surroundings seemed to dissolve and my feeling of separation vanished. In a strange way I felt blended into a total unity with the earth, as if I were made of it and it of me. I was aware of the blades of grass between my fingers and touching my face, and I was overwhelmed by a force which seemed to penetrate every fibre of my being.

'I felt as if I had suddenly come alive for the first time – as if I were awakening from a long deep sleep into a real world. I remember feeling that a veil had been lifted from my eyes and everything came into focus, although my head was still on the grass. Whatever else I believed, I realised that I was surrounded by an incredible loving energy, and that everything, both living and non-living, is bound inextricably with a kind of consciousness which I cannot describe in words.

'Although the experience could not have lasted for more than a few minutes, it seemed endless – as if I were in some kind of suspended eternal state of understanding. Then it passed and I remained still and quiet on the lawn, trying to absorb what had happened and not quite believing that it was real. A profound feeling of joy and peace is what I recall afterwards from those extraordinary moments.

'I felt totally incapable of discussing what had happened with anyone else at the time and didn't attempt to do so. Then – a few months later something similar happened, although in a different context.

'It was the following spring, again a bright warm day, and I was driving down a quiet country lane towards my home not far away. The road was a gentle slope downhill for about half a mile and I could see the dome of a mansion in the distance between the tops of the trees which were springing into leaf. I had a sudden flash once again of an incredible power surrounding me. I remember seeing the trees and fields flash by and my hands at the wheel.

'It was all over by the time I reached the T-Junction at the end of the lane where I had to turn right. The last half mile or so of my journey seemed quite normal, except that I had the same feeling of peace as on the previous occasion.

'These two experiences felt as if they were revelations, and that I had inexplicably tuned into some mysterious vibration of which I'd been unaware before. Since then I have read accounts of other people's experiences which seem similar in content and quality, but I've never discussed mine with anyone else, before writing this down. I've had many other versions of the same experience over the years – less intense, but still involving my whole self in this extraordinary way. Sometimes they seem to last for several hours, or even days at a time and I find my energy levels very high. I also feel in close contact with other people and my surroundings during these periods, and my thoughts and intuitions seem to be particularly sharp and in focus.

'. . . their general effect has been to enrich the quality of my life and to give me a sense of continuity and meaning which has taken me through times of great personal crisis, when it seemed that everything was crumbling away. From these experiences, I have also gained a profound sense of wonder and mystery about the earth and the universe we inhabit, and an ever-deepening respect for all of life.'

Another unsought experience is that of Muz Murray and it reveals all the characteristics of spontaneous mystic illumination. As in the preceding experience, this person was temperamentally hostile to spiritual concerns, but in his case it was a single, unrepeated experience that took place while he was hitch-hiking round the world that was to change his whole outlook.

'A loving hand inside my skull'
'One evening, in Cyprus, in 1964, I was sitting vacantly looking at the sea, in the afterglow of sunset, having just finished a meal in an old Greek eatery on the shore. I was feeling very tranquil and relaxed, when I began to feel a strange pressure in my brain. It was as if some deliciously loving hand had crept numbingly under my skull and was pressing

rain softly into mine. I felt a thrilling liquidity of being and an
able sensation as if the whole universe was being poured into
me, or rather, more as if the whole universe was welling-out of me from
some deep centre. My "soul" thrilled and swelled and kept expanding
until I found myself among and within the stars and planets. I understood
that I was the whole universe! Yet suddenly I became aware of huge
entities millions of miles high, manoeuvring in space, through which
the stars could still be seen.

'The all vision vanished as wave upon wave of extraordinary revelation
swept through me, too fast for my conscious mind to record other than
the joy and wonder of it. In those moments of eternity I lived and
understood the truth of the esoteric saying "as above – so below".
Every single cell in my "expanded body" – wherever the body was
during that bodiless experience – seemed to record and intuit everything
which occurred, retaining it like the negative film emulsion in a camera.
I was shown that every cell had its own consciousness which was mine.
And it seemed then that the whole of humanity was in the same condition:
each "individual" believing in his or her separate mind, but in reality still
subject to a single controlling consciousness – that of *Absolute
Consciousness Itself*.

'The awe and wonder of the things experienced were beyond my
imagination. It could not have lasted more than three minutes (or
maybe only one?) but it was enough to change my whole life. All the
following week I walked about in great happiness, with a crystal vision
which gave a greater luminosity to the air and all but made the people
and the buildings around me transparent. I wanted to embrace everyone
and tell them what happened and yet, paradoxically, I found myself
unwilling to profane the experience by attempting to express it in words
even to my closest friends. It was ten years before I could begin to speak
of it. Even now, sixteen years later, this is the first time I have spoken of
it – so profound was its effect on me.

'But my whole cocksure, intellectual assurance of how I imagined-
the-world-to-be, was destroyed in one go. I could no longer take anything
for granted. My character and lifestyle began to change. Without conscious
effort or intention, I found myself growing away from stimulants in my
diet, withdrawing from meat, alcohol and tobacco: a process which
seemed relative to the experience. I read everything I could lay my
hands on about mysticism, which I had previously disdained. From
being an agnostic and intense unbeliever, I was suddenly *On The Path!*'

This experience led Muz Murray to spend three years travelling to
the Sufi masters in India as a 'wandering pilgrim'. As a P.S. to his letter,

he says: 'Over the years, I have the impression that the information recorded in my cells, has been filtering through into awareness in mini-revelations from time to time.' (The subject of mini, or 'micro' illuminations is covered later in the book.)

The experience of C.G. Price, which follows, differs from the foregoing in two ways: firstly, it happened at a period when he was in great distress and felt out of control of his life, and secondly, he refers to sensing 'an unseen presence'. The experience left him with a sense of contentment, despite his problems, and a liberating and transforming mystic insight.

At the time, he was running a small-holding and was going through a period of great financial strain. Things were not going well, and he was not only 'very, very worried' but angry and bitter at the prospect of having to sell his farm and the animals on it – both of which he loved. 'I didn't want to lose them, they mattered to me, and I felt that God was not pulling his weight on my behalf.'

'A cocoon of golden light'
'With thoughts of self-pity such as these in my mind, one Sunday morning in February 1968, dreading the start of a new week with the possibility of more bad news and so on, I set about the task of bedding my cows down with straw. Shaking up bales of straw is not very demanding on the intellect, and I wasn't thinking about anything in particular that I can remember. I don't even remember the feeling creeping up on me, but quite suddenly . . .

'I seemed to be enveloped in a cocoon of golden light that actually felt warm, and which radiated a feeling of Love so intense that it was almost tangible. One felt that one could grasp handfuls of it, and fill one's pockets.

'In this warm cocoon of golden light I sensed a presence which I could not actually see but knew was there. My mind became crystal clear, and in an instant of time I suddenly knew, without any doubts, that I was part of a "Whole". Not an isolated part but an integral part. I felt a sense of "One-ment". I knew that I belonged and that nothing could change that. The loss of my farm and livelihood didn't matter any more. I was an important part of the "Wholeness" of things, and transient ambitions were secondary.

'How long this experience lasted I really don't know, probably only a few seconds, because when I "came to" again, I was still shaking up straw. There was, however, a sort of afterglow that lingered on for days, and even now, as I re-live the experience, that feeling of one-ness is as strong as ever.

'Eventually I did have to sell my farm, and give up the work I loved best. It no longer seemed important. There were other areas in life where I was needed, and where what few skills I do possess could be put to better use in the service of my brothers and sisters.'

He concludes: '. . . There is no doubt in my mind that since I underwent that experience, I have a greater inner contentment than I ever thought possible, and an enhancement of what I can only describe as quality of living. Things fall into perspective that much more easily, and what would hitherto have been major crises in my life no longer appear as such.'

Claire Myers Owens, who described herself as 'a privileged American housewife' also refers to 'a golden light' in the experience quoted next, which took place when she was sitting at her desk. Unlike C.G. Price, she did have forewarnings, in the form of 'small ecstasies', before she encountered what she calls 'the most frightening, beautiful, important experience of my entire life'.

Clair Myers Owens has had some extremely intense spontaneous mystic experiences and her descriptions and analyses of them have been incorporated in her book *Awakening to The Good*. Rather than considering her experiences beyond belief or worse, mad, her accounts caused enormous interest and response from well-known physicists and philosophers, and Abraham Maslow, whose self-actualisation movement was just commencing in 1958, gave her the names of 100 professors in universities all over the world whom he thought should be notified. She also received hundreds of warm and interested letters from 'professors, Hindus, Buddhists, Catholics, Jews, blacks, secretaries, housewives'.

At the time when this particular experience occurred, she was in considerable inward distress at the state of the world 'with its cold wars, world wars, atomic bombs, crime, corruption and lack of honor and integrity,' and illness had come and left her body weak for several months.

During these months, she had been benefited and uplifted by a series of small ecstasies that made her ask if they proved she possessed innate good? No, it felt to her more like an intimation of the 'existence of some transcendent power'.

'The grand purgation'
'Then the most incredible thing happened – the most frightening, beautiful, important experience of my entire life. I understood absolutely nothing

of its meaning at the time.

'One morning I was writing at my desk in the quiet writing room of our quiet house in Connecticut. Suddenly everything within my sight vanished right away. No longer did I see my body, the furniture in the room, the white rain slating across the windows. No longer was I aware of where I was, the day or hour. Time and space ceased to exist.

'Suddenly the entire room was filled with a great golden light, the whole world was filled with nothing but light. There was nothing anywhere except this effulgent light and my own small kernel of the self. The ordinary "I" ceased to exist. Nothing of me remained but a mere nugget of consciousness. It felt as if some vast transcendent force was invading me without my volition, as if all the immanent good lying latent within me began to pour forth in a stream, to form a moving circle with the universal principle. Myself began to dissolve into the light that was like a great golden all-pervasive fog. It was a mystical moment of union with the mysterious infinite, with all things, all people. . .

'It was the grand purgation, I was washed clean and pure like a sea shell by the mighty tides of the sea. All my personal problems fell away out of sight. My ego had drowned in boundless being. Irrefutable intimations of immortality came welling up. I felt myself becoming an indestructible part of indestructible eternity. All fear vanished – especially fear of death. I felt death would be the beginning of new more beautiful life . . .

'Extraordinary intuitive insights flashed across my mind. I seemed to comprehend the nature of things. I understood that the scheme of the universe was good, it was only man that was out of harmony with it. I was inherently good, not evil as our Western society had taught me as a child; all people were intrinsically good. Neither time nor space existed on this plane. I saw into the past and observed man's endless struggle toward the light. Love and suffering and compassion for the whole human race so suffused me that I knew I never again could condemn any person no matter what he or she did. I also saw into the distant future and beheld man awakening gradually to the good in himself, in others, moving with the harmonious rhythm of the universe, creating a new golden age – in some sweet tomorrow.

'How long this blissful state lasted – a minute, an hour – I shall never know. Just as suddenly I returned to consciousness. I did not know where I was, what time of day it was. I felt disoriented, as if I had been on a long trip to a distant strange country. The sight of my old desk and the blue couch was reassuring. But what on earth had happened to me? What did it all mean? Was I . . .losing my mind?

'Had the vivid reliving of all the "small ecstasies" of my entire life precipitated this mysterious rebirth? Or was it the natural sequence that followed psychological death of the ego? I did not know – then.'

Claire Myers Owens became convinced that over the years this revelation of 'cosmic consciousness' transformed her life, her character, and her relationships with all those close to her.

The distinguishing feature of the type of unexpected experience that follows is the activating role played by sound. Brenda Bunyon, who studied at the Royal School of Music, found that the vibrations of a Stradivarius led to a liberating perspective and to a specific inner prompting. She explained that she had been under severe emotional stress due to a traumatic domestic situation for about eight months prior to this experience about six years ago:

'Awe of the great mystery'
'This [mystical experience] was undoubtedly triggered off [note the use of the term] by the vibrating harmonics on a very fine violin, which was being played to me, a most beautiful Stradivarius. The blind eyes of my soul were gradually awakened from dormant sleep by the magnetic vibrations, at a very high frequency. I was aware of some great magnificent power spreading over and above me, lifting me upwards to another sphere, and I felt the awe of the great mystery. I could look down onto the whole world, and perceive humanity (like millions of busy little creatures) scampering about in their materialistic ways. Everything became incredibly clear – I could at once understand the universe as a whole, nature, the sea, the dark abyss, the great oceans – everything.

'In all this amazing vision, nothing appeared except as a divine power, a life force . . . in such a way as to be indescribable and I am only merely groping for words . . . I was bursting with fantastic joy and wonder, and constantly questioned my own sanity, because of such a state of mind. But this was no strange imagination or wanderings of imbalance.

'I was being urged to move in different directions, by invisible forces, utterly beyond my control. It seemed as if I was in the heavens themselves, and the inflow of joy is not at all possible to describe, except to say that all was good . . . Since then, my whole concept of life has changed – I have become deeply religious . . . .' (As one of the corollaries of her experience, Brenda Bunyon has pursued 'The Vibration of Sound' as a healing medium.)

Very different were the circumstances of Trevor Watts, a young Englishman who had left school at fifteen, tried his hand at various kinds of manual work but who was dissatisfied with his aimless existence and inability to find a meaning in life. The experience that follows was to provide him with self-enlightenment and a feeling of having been reborn. He was, he explained, at a low ebb when it suddenly happened.

'Life began making sense'

'I had returned to my bed-sit room in Earls Court after a day's work and knew I just couldn't go on in the way I was living. I cried out to the depths of my being and a great flood of energy came pouring in – such a power I had never felt before.

'I sat motionless for a while. I lost all sense of time. A great calm came to me like I never would have thought possible. Life began making sense to me. All the great truths that I'd heard and read became meaningful for the first time. I realised that if I wanted to change the world I must first change myself. I was looking in the mirror, my eyes were wide open, my face was like I had never seen it before. I was aglow, alive. I felt like It was just being born. It was a revelation but the height of awareness had not come to stay. It was not as easy as that – I had to earn it.'

Two years later, Trevor Watts again felt at breaking point. He had a second experience, occurring in his room as before, but this time it spread over several days and the effects were lasting: 'As I looked into the mirror my eyes appeared to be as white light – with no pupils. (Later, I was to learn that this experience lasted three days.) The curtains were drawn. Sometimes when I looked out it was dark, sometimes daylight, but it didn't seem to matter. It was as if time had ceased to exist. I did not sleep and ate next to nothing. I never felt the need of it. I had an image of a tree in my mind and all the branches represented the different paths I had traversed and came to dead ends. The branches began pulling in like they were growing backward into nothing, or ungrowing, until there was only one straight pathway ahead. Music was playing and I became it. The music and I were one. I felt what mystics have called "I am" and saw who I really was. I felt like I could never die and would always be.'

In contrast to Trevor's protracted experience, that of Major Haswell, a British officer in World War II, took place in no time at all, according to an observer, outside 'real' time altogether. In the face of almost certain death, he experienced revelation and a sense of oneness with all living things. This case is of a unique type among those quoted in that what happened to him on the spiritual plane appears to have had a direct consequence on the lives of his men.

'Bird song in Dante's Inferno'

'Whilst acting Gun Position Officer of a troop of 25-pounder Field Guns in Belgium in W.W.II, in support of the Grenadier Guards battalion, we were situated in a rather isolated farm . . . from which the farmer and family had fled, leaving all his cattle and livestock. The location of the farm was some miles north of Brussels. Soon after taking up our position we were subjected to heavy bombardment from a German Artillery Unit, whose Observation Post was in a church tower about a mile and a half away.

'After we had fired the required number of shells on our target the order was received to evacuate the position and move to another area. I gave the order for the tractors, which were in the farmyard, to move up to the guns which, during a lull in the German shelling, were to be manhandled into a position for hook-up and to be towed into position in the farmyard, ready to move off. As five of the guns were so moved and as the sixth was moving off an intense shelling of the No.1 gun position commenced. This gun and its position was nearest my control point and the gun was sited in a very large dung heap, and some 5 yards away from a slit trench, into which the gun team, my Gun Position Officer's Assistant . . . and I had now moved because of the shrapnel shells which were now exploding on the gun site.

'We were in full view of the German Observation Post and it was obvious that the tactics were to pin us down and prevent any movement. The scene was like Dante's Inferno with the shells coming in one after another and exploding about 3 feet above the ground, which made us crouch down in the slit trench. Cattle in the yard were being hit, horses which had been kept near us already had been killed. I now received an enquiry as to why I had not moved and, after explaining the situation, was given a direct order to move at once.

'I turned to the men with me and said "We have to move, and I don't think any of us will live in this, never mind reach the gun and manhandle it out of the dung heap and also the ammunition limber. I am going to say a prayer, and I would advise you all to make peace with God in your own way." The noise about us was deafening, the flash of flame, the smell of cordite and the manure being flung all about us. We could hear the white hot shrapnel hitting the gun, and the wall immediately to the right of us, and we expected to be cut to pieces as we emerged from the shelter to the slit trench.

'As I turned away from the men in order to pray I felt a tap on my

shoulder. It was my G.P.O. Assistant asking if I would pray fo
"as they did not know how to pray or what to say". I then asked
kneel — we were crouched — and I prayed to God asking forgiv
our sin in Christ our Lord and deliverance from what appeared to be
certain death. As soon as I said "Amen", I blew my whistle to signal the
gun tractor up, and shouted "let's go" at the same time scrambling out
of the slit trench.

'*Then something happened.*

'The moment I stood upright the sound of the shells exploding ceased,
but I still saw the flame of the explosions. But now there was a stillness,
and I could hear the song of birds, loud and quite close. (There were no
birds within miles of the farm!) Then I saw fluttering and hovering on the
dung heap at the side of the gun, a white cabbage butterfly. (I am sure
there were no butterflies either!) Then in a moment of time I *was* the
white butterfly! I was conscious of my being, of my wings moving,
especially so in the rate of beating of the wings.

'Then I became conscious of my vision from within my body as a
butterfly, and the action of my proboscis. Then I became intimately
conscious of my inner system, and the fluids moving therein because I
was the fluid and at the same time the containing vessels. Then I became
aware as it were, instantaneously, that I was now in the field, in front of
the farm, and all was peace, no sound, no flames, nothing only the field,
the sun, the trees and the sound of many birds trilling.

'Suddenly, then, in a flash, I was at the bottom of many blades of
grass — hundreds — all pulsing, thrusting upwards but exulting in a form
of soundless praise, as I had felt in the body of the butterfly, the reason
for its being, that it was in some way conscious of this itself, that there
was a creative dynamic outside of itself, yet intimately connected with
it, so I felt the same with the grass roots, they were literally alive and in
tune with the Universe of which they formed a part.

'There was I, an actual blade of grass, but unlike a blade of grass,
conscious of exactly what I was, and what I was doing and my relationship
to the cellular make-up of the earth in which I was and to other myriad
blades of grass.'

Major Harwell describes what happened afterwards:

'In an instant all changed. I was running forward immediately from
the edge of the slit trench, my men clambering out behind me! I again
blew my whistle for the tractor to come up, but the driver made no
move, he was afraid to do so I learned later. I then sent the bombardier
down to bring the tractor gun tower up together with the driver. I
assisted the men to move the gun and ammunition limber into position

for hook-up. Whilst this was in process the shells were still actually exploding about us! When the tractor arrived the canvas top was cut by shrapnel.

'During all this chaos one event remains vividly in my memory. It was one of the gun team on the opposite side of the tractor to me shouting "It's a bloody miracle!" We hooked up and proceeded to the head of the 6 gun column. Not a single man had received as much as a scratch . . . We were fired on as we proceeded down the roadway to our destination, not a vehicle or gun being hit.'

Most extraordinary to Major Haswell was that this moment of total molecular oneness, of 'noiseless sound', of being a vibrating part of universal life that was 'beyond description,' is that as far as the bombardier could see Major Haswell had never halted long enough for such a moment to have occurred. After jumping out of the slit trench he had just kept running on to the gun, not pausing until he had reached it. After which the men gathered round him to 'thank God'.

Major Haswell had been predisposed to religion, which was why he had acted as the 'padre' in this situation; after being discharged from the Army, he became a Reader in the Anglican Church for 27 years until his retirement.

Irina Starr, an American teacher and writer who lives and works in the Greater Los Angeles area of California, has recorded her extraordinary and prolonged mystic experiences in a remarkable book, *The Sound of Light* (1974). Although the 'primary thrust of her life' had been spiritual, Irina Starr felt that these experiences, in their power and intensity, brought her back to her essential self after 'a long unhappy detour'. The segment covered in her book is a seven-year span from mid-1955 to mid-1962 and includes several major transcendental experiences, spontaneous and unsought, one of four days' duration and a series which extended over a 42-day period. It is difficult to do justice to the quality of sustained bliss conveyed by the whole account, but the following passage, taken from the beginning of her mystical state of four days' duration, illustrates its overwhelming power. She is describing here how the familiar objects in her bedroom seemed to her as she opened her eyes one morning.

'Everything was literally alive'

'The radiance which permeated my eyelids and suffused the entire room caught me unawares. Everything around me had come to life in some wondrous way and was lit from within with a moving, living, radiance.

It was somewhat as it must be with one blinded, whose vision is first restored.

'I was obviously seeing with vision other than the purely physical, but what I saw did not conflict with what my ordinary vision registered any more than the central vision conflicts with the peripheral; or close, medium, and far ranges of vision conflict one with the other. I saw objects in the ordinary way as well as with some extraordinary extension of the visual faculty; I saw into them with an inner vision and it was this inner sight which revealed the commonplace objects around me to be of the most breath-taking beauty. By an almost unconscious act of will, as when one switches from one range of vision to another, I found that I brought the inner luminosity into a more intense focus and the ordinary appearance of things receded into a sort of secondary vision. The latter occupied a position in my vision at some undetermined point which was neither peripheral nor a recognized range, but some new point for which I had no frame of reference. By a reverse action, the change took place as swiftly as a reflex, and the ordinary vision took sharp focus while the luminous vision remained out of focus and at the new intermediate point, suffusing all, but not focussed upon anything in penetration.

'I was literally transfixed as my gaze rested upon first one thing and then another; my hand upon the bedspread, the maple table beside the bed, the dust which rested lightly upon it, the telephone, the flowers in a vase, the several books. There was the luminous quality – a light which contained color in the way that a brilliant diamond refracts color, only this color seemed an integral part of the essential substance and not a form of refracted light. The one thing which was, above all, significant was that everything was literally alive; the light was living, pulsating, and in some way I could not quite grasp, intelligent. The true substance of all I could see was this living light, beautiful beyond words. This awareness of beauty so intense as to be nearly unbearable was not to leave me for four days in which I beheld the world with extended sight.

'As I gazed about the room on that first morning, one of the things which particularly fascinated me was that there was no essential difference between that which was inanimate – only in form and function, not in basic substance, for there was only the one Substance, that living, knowing, Light which breathed out from everything. I was aware of the outward difference of each object which drew my attention, but that superficial difference in no way concealed or conflicted with the one substance or living light which composed each alike. Ever since I could remember, I had accepted the fact of one-ness of all life and manifestation, but it was purely theoretical, an intellectually accepted condition. But here I was literally beholding the fact itself so very far beyond any concept I had ever held.

'There was such beauty in all that met my eyes that I could have remained for hours gazing at any one thing and the feelings of joy and wonder were so strong they seemed to generate a peculiar pain. I recall that I was near-bursting with a tremendous, non-conceptual, understanding of life – like a balloon which expanded to its utmost capacity – so that my mind was strained with this great, formless "knowing" and I actually prayed, *Enough!* . . .

'I knew that I could never explain or transmit verbally the essence of what was transpiring in my consciousness, I could only *be* the truth, the living expression of inner revelation, and as such it would be transmitted in its own way, beyond my knowing or intent . . . It is a wondrous and mysterious sort of divine chemical process which takes place in the human and his orbit as truth moves from concept into living experience. We are holy factories in more ways than one.'

By the end of her seventh day of these life-shaking experiences, Irina Starr says 'I was not the same person I had been one short week before. Nor could I ever experience my world again but in a new and revelatory manner; I had emerged into a dawn-fresh and excitingly life-filled dimension.'

Hers may well be the longest record of contemporary mystic experience, but many of the very short, single-flash experiences are like portions of Irina Starr's, recognisably the same.

Far from being of a contemplative turn of mind, Jim Harrison paid little attention to spiritual matters until he had the experience that follows – one which he interprets as proof of the nature of God and which left him with a complete change of view and a profound sense of enlightenment. He had left England at 18 to go to Zimbabwe and grow tobacco, and except for the war years when he flew reconnaissance aircraft in the Middle East and Italy, had been there ever since. At the time of his mystic experience, he explained, he was 'thinking some hard thoughts' about a Deity that would ignore his wife's fervent prayers for improved health.

'A brilliant shaft of light'
Then he began to wonder: ' . . . Suppose that I were God, and that I had made a tiny little rock, mud and water ball, set it in a vast universe, and populated it with teeming millions of people, giving them free will to do entirely as they pleased, perhaps it might be the exercise

of this free will that caused the misfortunes that we suffer?

'Maybe it wasn't really God's fault after all! So then I thought all right, I take it all back, and filling my heart with the tender love often reserved for my little daughter, I projected it towards him, thinking, if you exist then I give you my love.'

It was then that he had the following experience:

'. . . I could feel this love being passed on and on, and then suddenly it returned − a brilliant shaft of light from out of the sky, brighter by far than the mid-morning sun, permeating me with such an intensity of happiness and Love as to halt me in my tracks with a jump for joy − and lingering for five or ten seconds before fading away. I knew intuitively that this light, plainly visible, extending into the sky, somehow, mysteriously, stemmed from within.

'So then I knew for certain that God does indeed exist, that he is love, that he is joy, that he is light, that he stems from within as much as from without, and that we alone are responsible for our own sufferings and problems in consequence of the mis-use of our free will.

'That was many years ago now and though I have since had different experiences of our Creator, I cannot imagine why I should have been so singularly fortunate, except perhaps to share such experiences with others.'

Few of the foregoing accounts have been couched in specifically Christian terms but when Moyra Caldecott, a 'nervous, giggly' schoolgirl, received her brief moment of illumination she interpreted it as the 'descent of the Dove', i.e. the reception of the Holy Spirit, third person of the Christian Trinity.

Growing up in South Africa in a Christian, church-going household she realises on looking back that she probably never questioned her belief − nor did she believe. Most of the time she was bored during the Services, and annoyed to have to give up sweets in Lent. The particular day that changed her feelings was during the preparation for her Confirmation, which was just 'something we all did at that age, and I was more interested in the pretty white dress my mother made for me for the occasion than in the meaning of the words I could so glibly quote.'

'The magnificent glimpse'
'We girls in our white dresses sat in the front pew − the boys with their hair slicked down and looking remarkably uncomfortable on the opposite aisle. We had rehearsed how we had to go up one by one and kneel at the

altar rail. The Bishop of Natal had come to Pietermaritzburg specially to perform the ceremony. I didn't really look at him. He was all cased in a long cape and tall hat and seemed very remote. We were nervous and giggly. What if we did something wrong?

'The service went on and I, as usual, was only half aware of it. My mouth was opening and shutting, saying the expected words, but my thoughts were all over the place – certainly not on anything profoundly religious.

'The time came for us to file up to the altar rail and kneel down. I did so. Not expecting anything. Noticing how prickly the kneeling cushion was on my knees. Waiting for the Bishop to reach me. He was muttering something and putting his hand on each one's head in turn.

'It was my turn. He put his hand on my head . . .

'I didn't hear what he said but . . . And this is an experience I would like to describe but find it almost impossible to do so.

'I suddenly seemed to cease to be me (that is, in the sense of "me" I had thought I was – living in a particular house, in a particular street, going to a particular school). I felt the most incredible flow of energy and power coursing through me and had, what I believe to be, an experience of Timeless Reality . . . of consciousness that took in everything without limit . . . but reacted to nothing except in the sense of "knowing . . . and . . . "loving".

'The Bishop must have had his hand on my head for no more than a few seconds – but one could live a whole lifetime and not gain as much insight as I gained in this one beautiful, devastating moment.

'I stood up and went back to my place in the pew as I had been trained to do . . . trembling, shaken . . . remembering the description of John baptising Jesus and the Love of the Holy Spirit descending . . . so *that* is what that meant! Could something similar have happened to me? I was terrified. If it had happened . . . really happened . . . then all that Christ said in the Bible was *true*, not just something one was expected to believe but didn't.

'The rest of the service passed without my noticing it. I was in turmoil and after that day for a while I read the Bible not because I was told to, but because I was eager to understand what it was teaching.'

Twenty years passed. Moyra Caldecott married a publisher, had children, did not think too deeply about the meaning of life, except when she had occasional amazing flashes of disturbing insight. Later, she became ill with angina, and after another mystic experience which confirmed for her the whole of mystical philosophy so that she accepted it with 'all my heart', she was healed.

'I know I cannot yet answer all the questions I would like to, but one thing I am sure of – and that is that there *is* a Mystery at the core of existence that analytical science alone has not and cannot solve for us. The magnificent glimpse, the moment of illumination, more precious than gold, rarer than moon-rock, is probably the only way we will ever be able to approach it.'

The experience of Dorothy Gowenlock, another teenaged girl at the time, is interesting to compare with the previous one. Her mystical state occurred when she was depressed at 'the world's woes', and it was never repeated; although brief, it had the same unmistakable impact.

'Surrounded by vivid light'

'I came to the 23rd of February, 1948, in a state which I didn't know about, being young, that I know now as "the dark night of the soul". I sat dejected and absolutely lost on a wet, cold Monday afternoon. I, for some reason, looked at the clock opposite to me and knew it was 3 p.m. . . . Suddenly my great anguish vanished and I felt free of earthly bonds of time and space and was absolutely surrounded, around me and within myself, by vivid light . . . and though I didn't see anyone, I felt a deep sense of love such as I had never before known. As soon as I could I went to bed and there I lay in a state of unadulterated bliss which lasted for hours.

'Easter Sunday following this experience I started to walk to church, and as I looked at some grasses waving in the wind, I felt at one with the world and everything in it – the waving grass, birds singing, myself, all seemed to have formed a complete whole. This feeling didn't last for long, but whilst it did it was delightful. I continued my walk to church, my first walk in that direction for five years . . .

'I have never had another experience since.'

This last spontaneous mystic experience differs from all the rest in being recorded by a witness rather than by the person who experienced it. What follows is a transcript of what actually took place, in the presence of several hundred people. Ernest Holmes, the leader of a New Thought Movement in America called *Religious Science*, was, in 1959, the principal speaker at the dedication of a new Church in California. As often happened in giving talks, his voice would take on an inspired tone, but on this occasion his inspiration became extremely intense, there was a distinct change in his voice – and he abruptly ended his talk. These were the last actual words of his talk, and the way in which they expressed what he was experiencing *as he was experiencing it:*

'Mingling with the hosts of heaven'
'...We are dedicated to the concept that the pure in heart shall see God, here; that the meek will inherit the earth, now; that one with Truth is a majority; that every one of us in the secret place of the most High, in the center of his own consciousness, has the secret with the Eternal, the Everlasting, the Almighty, and the Ineffable. God and I are One. And I see uniting in one great inner praise, one great union of effort, one crescendo of song, and one enveloping light of consciousness...'

There was now a 12-second pause.

'I see it!' (A hushed but dynamic voice)

And now a 10-second pause.

'O God!'

A five-second pause.

'The veil is thin between.'

Pause.

'We do mingle with the hosts of heaven.'

Pause.

'I see it!

'And I shall speak no more.'

Witnesses at the time said Ernest Holmes appeared radiant, but though he spoke of the experience to a friend, he never made public mention of it.

Of course, it is not possible to record here exactly what Ernest Holmes was experiencing, and such moments were not put under scrutiny but left very much alone as a purely personal matter. Perhaps his audience were carried with him in a nameless way: or they may have thought he had been carried away in an extreme of religious fervour. Only that it was some kind of a mystic experience of a spontaneous nature remains.

A Closer Look at the Trigger-Factor

> 'I became aware of something in me which flashes upon my reason. I perceive of it that it is something but what it is I cannot conceive. Only meseems that, could I conceive it, I should comprehend all truth' – Meister Eckhart

In the majority of accounts of spontaneous mystic experience, past or present, a kind of antecedent situation or condition is given. People speak of what they were doing, feeling, where they were in the moments before the lightning shift of focus from ordinary to extraordinary reality took place. 'I was just doing such-and-such,' they will say, or 'just thinking so-and-so, when *suddenly* . . .!'

What happened then, may or may not be seen as a result, or to have arisen from, that particular antecedent condition. In her book *Ecstasy* (1961), Marghanita Laski proposed the idea that some causative set of circumstances acted like a 'trigger' to alter the perception of the experiencer, and that this 'trigger-factor' could be traced and classified.

This proposition has certainly provided a convenient terminology for the attempt to categorise the special circumstances that possibly give rise to the 'tearing aside of a veil', as well as potential clues to the very nature of mystic experience itself.

Interestingly, without knowing of the coined term, a great many people in recent times themselves use the word 'trigger', saying '. . .something seemed to trigger this feeling. . .' or 'the experience seemed to be triggered by . . .': the circumstances appear to have the literal effect of *setting off* the burst of illumination, of being the *activating means* or mechanism.

In an exploration of this trigger-factor, then, the main questions seem to be: just how consistent is it in all accounts; to what extent can they be categorised; and if they *can* all be classified, does some form of revelation emerge which casts significant light on the phenomenon of spontaneous mystic experience?

From a look at several hundreds of experiences, the impression is of several distinct categories that begin to sound very familiar, and with which almost anyone who has had ecstatic moments – apart from the 'the joy unspeakable', as the medieval mystic Hugh of St Victor called his interior heights, '. . .this thing of delight, that moves me with such sweetness and violence that I am drawn out of myself and carried away, I know not how. . .' – may recognise and relate to with ease. Some of these (not all named, a few anonymous) are as follows:

'It flashed up lightning-wise *during a performance of Beethoven's Seventh Symphony at the Queen's Hall* . . .in that triumphant fast movement when "the morning stars sang together and all the sons of God shouted for Joy" ', wrote Warner Allen, an agnostic journalist in his book *The Timeless Moment* (1946).

Concerts, operas, melodic, nostalgic or even wildly rhythmic music are probably the most often-quoted trigger-factor. It seems as if music touches off the well-spring of mystic rapture, as if sound reaches a certain mysterious order within the inner aspects of being and transports human reality to a higher dimension.

Response to the beauties of Nature is also given with such frequency that it has lent itself to a whole classification of its own – 'Nature Mysticism'.

'It was one of those gloriously lovely days that one sometimes sees in England – a cloudless vividly blue sky with brilliant sunshine. It was morning. The air was shimmering with the moisture from the evaporating dew. I was walking on the lawn looking at the masses of flowers in the herbaceous border. As a gardener I was interested in what was coming up into flower; as an artist I was enjoying the combination of colour, light and shade. Suddenly, as I paused in contemplation, I was "lifted" into another world (plane or dimension?) . . .' The quotation is from *Watcher on the Hills*, by Raynor C. Johnson.

Again and again, this type of trigger-situation relates to walks in the woods, the beauty of skies, trees, flowers, a flight of birds, a certain stillness at dusk or dawn, a pearly light over a village, a sweeping view of beautiful countryside, the sea in various moods, a mountain top: and in this rapport with the basic elements of all life, it is not hard to believe that it could extend itself into mystic transport.

Further than these more obvious antecedent conditions, are some that are less often recorded, but frequently enough to lend themselves to classification:

Childbirth: Rapture of knowing the child has been born. Joy of first contact. Thankfulness. Fulfillment. Sense of being part of a universal process. Protectiveness. Meaning.

Sports: Exhilaration. Forgetfulness of body, time, place in all-out exertion, moving only to a goal. Singleness of purpose. Physical 'glow'.

Dedication: Full commitment to a work or creative pursuit that frees the 'daily' mind. Absorption that fuses mind and body.

Worship: Awe. Reverence. Immanence of 'Holy' presence. Surrender. Identification with religious figure. Intense compassion. Sense of 'Grace'.

The senses: Touch – softness, smoothness, the fur of an animal. Rhythm. Movement. Vibration. Aromas and fragrances. Variations of light and shade. Eye contact. The message of an expression. Seeing into 'the nature of things'. Breathing in a relaxed way. Well-being. Orgasm. Pleasant tastes.

Gratitude: Relief from pressure, worry, fear, pain. For love, help, a second chance or reprieve. For attainment, a gift, freedom, release.

Happiness: For oneself. For others. For being alive. A sense of blessedness. Self-acceptance. Forgiveness. Letting-go of the past, or of a grudge. Renewal. Hope. Love for all. An image of brotherhood, of world peace.

Achievement: Fulfillment. Satisfaction. Triumph. Arrival. Sense of expansion.

Flight: Unfettered space. Freedom from earthly and physical limitation. Freedom from the body in dream. Gliding. Flying in or operating aircraft. Speed. Acceleration to great heights.

Of course, there are many more, still less distinct: such as the trusting hand of a small child thrust into one's own; the loving companionship of an animal; kindred feeling for all creatures; love, in many aspects, sexual union, first enchantment, deep closeness, moment of being married; liberation from restrictions, mental or physical.

But as well as these positive triggers, there are negative ones, antecedent situations that are not so readily associated with the subsequent upsurge of joy. Among these are:

News of terminal illness: Denial, anger, withdrawal, may precede a sudden transition to 'eternal vision' – a life-is-but-a-learning-process release. A sense that the body has been a vehicle of instruction, that the spirit is untouched.

Pre-operative loneliness: Black despair may suddenly be lightened with the sense of a loving presence, peace, protection, understanding, trust.

Suicidal feelings: Suddenly, unexpectedly vanquished and replaced by overwhelming illumination of a goodness and purpose, of love and care from an invisible but real source.

Clinical death: Experience while heart is arrested of immense radiance, of peace, of going towards love and freedom – regret for return to 'ordinary' conditions. (Gerald Jampolski and Elizabeth Kubler Ross, psychologists whose main work and writing is concerned with terminally ill children, report that these children seem equipped with this mystic immanence, seldom feel the fear that adults are feeling, and frequently comfort their parents rather than seeking comfort from them.) See also *Bliss and Death*, p. 158.

In the midst of grief, loss, threat to life, shock, agony: Sudden peace, detachment, seeing the logic and order of the laws of life. Compassion or love for the enemy. Immunity to bodily fear. Oneness that transcends the ignorance of violence, the blindness of man's inhumanity to man. Sense of absolute inseparability from the 'allness' of being. Conversion to God or an omnipotent force seen or experienced as omnipresent and benevolent.

Besides these seemingly negative trigger-factors are many unlikely objects and sights that have been recorded often quite inexplicably. Reported as antecedent to the liberating exaltation, have been: the sight of a junk-heap or garbage dump; slime; excrement; derelict buildings; a dead chicken; fog; a wailing whistle in the dark; tears. The wonder of transformation following such antecedents can only intensify the mystery and leaves very little solid evidence for pinpointing the common denominator, if any, in the conditions appearing to precipitate mystic experience.

Perhaps there is no particular trigger-factor, only one or another situation, thought or feeling that happens to precede the explosion of light, which can in fact simply be anything at all and bears no relation whatever to the experience. On the other hand, perhaps there *is* a factor that triggers the onslaught of bliss but it as yet eludes definition, or even recognition. Perhaps like everything else in the evolution of human understanding, it has yet to be unfolded to awareness. Then it will be seen to have been in plain sight all the time.

Meanwhile, this very intriguing and puzzling aspect of mystic experience, which might well hold a significant key to its causation, offers a challenge to further exploration.

The Question of Ineffability

'When I undertake to tell the
best I find I cannot,
My tongue is ineffectual on
its pivots,
My breath will not be obedient
to its organs,
I become a dumb man'
        – Walt Whitman

Throughout all accounts of mystic experience there is one common claim: that the experience so far exceeds the bounds of language that it simply cannot be properly communicated, that it is 'ineffable'. Jacob Boehme (1575-1624), the inspired German shoemaker whose interpretations of mystic experience profoundly influenced the philosophy and history of mysticism, did not find it easier than those with similar experience today:

'...Who can express it?.... Or why and what do I write, whose tongue but does stammer like a child which is learning to speak? With what shall I compare it? Or to whom shall I liken it? Shall I compare it with the love of this world? No, that is but a mere dark valley to it.... O immense Greatness! I cannot compare it with any thing, but only with resurrection from the dead; there will the Love-Fire rise up again in us, and rekindle again our astringent, bitter, and cold, dark and dead powers, and embrace us most courteously and friendly.'

Unless one has had the experience he speaks from, how can these words be comprehended? Even if language could be stretched and expanded far beyond its current boundaries, would it ever be subtle or flexible enough to convey the experience itself?

Mystical experience is not alone, of course, in presenting problems of communication. When one considers the difficulty of describing even normal, everyday experiences to someone who cannot share them – the colour of a sunset to a blind person, the sound of a clarinet to someone who is deaf, precisely what it is like to fall in love to someone who has not felt this emotion – the immensity of the task of conveying mystical experience in words becomes apparent. (The writer quoted below, however, makes an interesting distinction between the problem of communicating such 'normal' experiences and that inherent in putting mystical experiences into words.)

In his book *The Invisible Writing,* Arthur Koestler wrote of experiences he had while a prisoner in a condemned cell during the Spanish Civil War. The trigger had been what he considered to be reconfirmed proof of Euclid's premise that the number of prime numbers is infinite, which the author believed he attained in figures scratched on the wall with a piece of wire:

'The significance of this,' he said, 'swept over me like a wave. The wave had originated in an articulate verbal insight; but this evaporated at once, leaving in its wake only a wordless essence, a fragrance of eternity, a quiver of the arrow in the blue. I must have stood there some minutes, entranced, with a wordless awareness that "this is perfect – perfect"; until I noticed some slight mental discomfort nagging at the back of my mind – some trivial circumstance that marred the perfection of the moment. Then I remembered the nature of that irrelevant annoyance: *I* was of course in prison and might be shot. But this was immediately answered by a feeling whose verbal translation would be: "So what? Is that all? Have you got nothing more serious to worry about?" – an answer so spontaneous, fresh and amused as if the intruding annoyance had been the loss of a collar-stud. Then I was floating on my back in a river of peace, under bridges of silence. It came from nowhere and flowed nowhere. Then there was no river and no I. The I had ceased to exist.

'When I say "the I had ceased to exist" I refer to a concrete experience that is verbally as incommunicable as the feeling aroused by a piano concerto, yet just as real – only much more real. In fact its primary mark is the sensation that this state is more real than any other one has experienced before – that for the first time the veil has fallen and one is in touch with "real reality", the hidden order of things, the X-ray texture of the world, normally obscured by layers of irrelevancy.

'What distinguishes this type of experience from the emotional entrancements of music, landscapes or love is that the former has a definitely intellectual, or rather noumenal [relating to the reality that underlies the visible world of phenomena] content. It is meaningful, though not in verbal terms. Verbal transcriptions that come nearest to it are: the unity and interlocking of everything that exists, an inter-dependence like that of gravitational fields or communicating vessels. The "I" ceases to exist because it has, by a kind of mental osmosis, established communion with, and been dissolved in, the universal pool. It is this process of dissolution and limitless expansion which is sensed as the "oceanic feeling", as the draining of all tension, the absolute catharsis, the peace that passeth all understanding . . . there remained a sustained and invigorating, serene and fear-dispelling after-effect that lasted for hours and days.'

'These experiences', Koestler added, 'filled me with a direct certainty that a higher order of reality existed, and that it alone invested existence with meaning.'

As articulate as this careful account was, there is still an incommunicable core (as there is in the attempt to share any personal experience, but more so in the mystic) that while it may stir the imagination, may be felt vicariously, undoubtedly falls far short of the experience.

In many of the contributions to this book, there was emphatic confession of inadequacy in the relating of the experience (these in some cases for reasons of space had to be condensed or even omitted). In some there was more than the usual embarrassment for any lack of skill with words, as though it was felt that more and higher education might have enabled greater fluency. Yet some of the simplest accounts, by their very inarticulateness conveyed stronger intimations of what had occurred, while the reaching for prose of equal beauty to the illumination sometimes created an artificial effect, as if the writer strove to use the language of the mystic to convince others the experience was in the recognisable mode.

In both cases there is evidence of the frustration of communicating another kind of reality that exists at every level of expression. Some people wrote to say that not only could they not put into words the immensity of their mystic experience, but felt it too sacred to expose to the limitations of language. Very often it was felt that language demeaned the experience. Some tried hard to tell it, and then abandoned the effort as hopeless. One man who had wished to be included, said, 'No matter how I wrote it, it always turned out to be shallow, lifeless and a lie.' What he could put on paper was the *effect*: '. . . Since my first shattering mystical experience six years ago, my life has been spent, to every "awakening" instant, in transforming myself.' Quoting the American social scientist Timothy Leary in *Neuropolitics*, who wrote: 'Larvas do not understand butterfly language', he added, 'I was a butterfly for a short time. I learned butterfly language. I just cannot translate it into larval language'.

Speaking of possible explanations for this difficulty, F.C. Happold, in *Mysticism*, says: '. . . our language has evolved primarily as an instrument for describing experience through the five senses. It does not lend itself easily to descriptions of rare spiritual and psychological states, which, though they may be states of knowledge, are also states of feeling. Like the poet and the musician, the mystic has to find a language of his own; it is to a great extent a language of symbols, and it is of the nature of symbolism that it conceals as well as reveals.'

But it is not only that language may be too sense-channelled to encompass these 'rare' states, but understanding on the intellectual or reasoning level may also be unable to accommodate the concepts of mystic experience. Perhaps symbolism is a substitute for that which is beyond conceptualisation. If the experience cannot be described while in process, then any description after the event must be one of attempted recall, which means that reason has to grapple with concepts that may be essentially untranslatable. It seems logical to assume that an experience of 'oneness' would mean that words, the tools of reason, would only cause separation into partiality, the 'undifferentiated' into differences in which all concepts fragment.

Perhaps this is why the word 'unspeakable' is so often used in descriptions of mystic experience, and why many Eastern gurus tell their pupils not to try to convey it, and why a principle of saying what it is *not*, the *via negativa*, or 'Negative Way', became such a widespread device among early mystics. Here, for instance, is a famous example taken from the writings of Dionysius the Areopagite (c. 500 AD), a Christian whose actual identity is obscure but whose doctrines (not all negative) have had considerable influence on mystical theology throughout the ages:

'Once more, ascending yet higher, we maintain It is not soul, or mind, or endowed with the faculty of imagination, conjecture, reason, or understanding; nor is It any act of reason or understanding; nor can It be described by the reason or perceived by the understanding, since It is not number, or order, or greatness, or littleness, or equality, or inequality, and since It is not immovable nor in motion, nor at rest, and has no power, and is not power or light, and does not live, and is not life; nor is It personal essence, or eternity, or time, nor can It be grasped by the understanding, since It is not knowledge or truth; nor is It kingship or wisdom; nor is It one, nor is It unity; nor is It Godhead or Goodness; nor is It a Spirit, as we understand the term, since It is not Sonship or Fatherhood; nor is It any other thing such as we or any other being can have knowledge of; nor does It belong to the category of non-existence; nor do existent beings know It as It actually is, nor does It know them as they actually are; nor can the reason attain to It to name It or know It; nor is It darkness, nor is It light; nor error; nor truth; nor can any affirmation or negation apply to to It; for while applying affirmations or negations to those orders of being that come next to It, we are not applying to It either affirmation or negations, inasmuch as It transcends all affirmation by being the perfect and unique Cause of all things, and transcends all negation by the preeminence of its simple and absolute nature.'

This approach paves the way for the *via affirmativa*, which then shows that while these are the qualities mystic experience is *not*, the qualities that *are*, exceed them into a luminescence and sublimity that cannot be worded but only *known*. This frequently leads to the use of paradox, those subtle contradictions that slip between the intellect and intuition like swift arrows of light to a centre of wordless understanding; and of metaphor, the oblique approach to description that implies what is not stated, employing resemblances and comparisons to create what Rudolf Otto in his book *The Idea of the Holy* called a 'numinous' quality, the sense of the experience itself.

In answer to a question by a student regarding what of ultimate transcendent reality could be expressed in words, Hsi Yun, a Zen master who lived in about 840 AD said: 'The nature of mind, when understood, no human words can encompass or disclose. Enlightenment is naught to be obtained, and he that gains it does not say he knows.' He added: 'If I were to make this clear to you, I doubt if you could stand up to such knowledge.'

Surrendering all analytical effort, giving up thought about that which defies language is the Eastern solution to the riddle. Turning from outer conceptualisation to absolute inner stillness without reason, intellect or the frantic leaping about of 'the monkey mind', brings insight of a profound and universal nature. Words are no longer needed, except as a means to teach and share, to help others toward their own experience of the mystic. Gurus far advanced along this path may go beyond verbal communication altogether and retreat into 'silence'. Occasionally, teachers of rare and compassionate wisdom will eschew silence in order to stay among the as-yet-unenlightened and continue to communicate what they know.

Dr Charles Musès, Director of Research at the Centre de Recherches en Mathematiques et Morphologie in Switzerland and co-author with Arthur Young of *Consciousness and Reality*, has a broadly cohesive viewpoint on the question of ineffability. He says: 'It was and is. . . . much easier to say that there is no way to express something than to find a way to communicate such meanings to those who are not yet aware of them . . .

'. . . Since the nature of the cosmos recedes into infinite orders of infinitesimals or infinites on all sides, there is an ever-present component of ineffability which denotes the unconstructability of the infinite. This ineffability is a hallmark of life itself, with its characteristic ever-newness.

'But this necessary ineffability of livingness must by no means be confused with any general or absolute limit upon communicability. For the other side of the coin of life reads that as long as man continues to experience he will be able to learn how to communicate that which previously was impossible for him to conceptualize or articulate. We are thus assured of two things: the impossibility of communicating all that reality contains at any given moment, but the possibility of communicating this at some future moment, by which time reality would again have outstripped our ability to communicate.'

To sum up this aspect of mystic experience for the purpose of an exploration, it would seem that the very struggle itself, to express in whatever way, and to whatever limits language can obtain, is the main significance. If vast numbers of people describe their experiences in approximately the same groups of phrases over and over again, so that despite the differences of time, place, social or religious conditioning the similarities stand out like beacons in the mist, then there is reason to suspect that the beacons could be extended and the mist rolled back.

4
Bliss as Induced Experience

'If one wants to find out what lies beyond the frontier, the only way to do so is to go beyond it and see. On this journey one will do well to obtain both a map and a guide but one will have to travel every step by one's own efforts' – Robert S. De Ropp, *The Master Game* (1968)

By far the greater proportion of mystic transcendence is intentionally sought – as opposed to those experiences that happen spontaneously – and by such a variety of methods that to enumerate them all would be almost impossible. Practices for the attainment of an altered state of consciousness that extends from the normal one of waking to some form of ecstasy, rapture or trance, reach back into antiquity. Every tribe and community of man throughout the world has expressed this apparent need with orgiastic rituals, rhythmic and repetitive bodily movements, prolonged shouting, screaming, singing, chanting, intoning, howling, withholding breath or periodic inhalation and exhalation, extreme ascetic disciplines such as protracted fasting, flagellation, the ingestion of consciousness-altering plants, and deprivation of sleep and the senses.

Although the methods may have changed with the evolution of societies, the basic element of inducement remains: somehow or other to reach out beyond the confines of ordinary reality, from transience and the ephemeral to something which lies waiting in the unknown, in the whole order of things. Evidence that there is this something has been sufficiently related and attested to, individual glimpses and intimations have given sufficient promise for it to be worth whatever the price of seeking, from Christian 'God-realisation' to Hindu *'Sat-Chit-Ananda'*, Being-awareness-Bliss.

What, then, are some of the surviving, existent and experimental ways of attempting to induce and develop experience of the mystic?

In broadest and most familiar terms, there is contemplative prayer

– the effort of direct communication with the Deity, which constitutes the mystical rather than purely theological element of almost all religions. This element, largely submerged in theology, is becoming increasingly emphasised these days and is sometimes called 'The New Mysticism', in that it crosses the boundaries between specific doctrines and dogmas to a common underlying root or original base.

There is meditation, basically indigenous to the East, but increasingly adopted by the West, in a wide variety of forms and techniques, and by far the most prevalent inducement of mystic Bliss.

And there are the drugs that chemically alter consciousness, some of ancient use and origin, some of recent development in which mystic experience has emerged indirectly in the course of initial experiment for other purposes.

In the first two categories, there is overlapping, for the line between contemplation and meditation is often too subtle for precise demarcation; either may induce mystic experience. Both require an attentive focus, a stilling of the mind, but whereas contemplation may be a deep thinking 'about', a profound consideration 'of' a subject, meditation is the quelling of thought altogether. This is achieved by means such as a 'mantra' (a word or sentence repeated over and over) or other devices such as Dervish Dancing in which thought is silenced by repetitive and sustained whirling; by steady and rhythmic breathing, in which the attention is centred on the breathing and nothing else, or by focusing the attention on a light, object or sound, or on some form of imagery such as a mandala, a kind of mystical diagram used in Hindu and Buddhist meditation.

'In its beginning,' the Indian philosopher Krishnamurti says, 'Meditation is an exercise in control of attention... Attention has no border, no frontier to cross; attention is clarity, clear of all thought. Thought is the cessation of meditation; good meditation begins with the cessation of thought. Awareness of this is to be attentive.... Meditation is not an intellectual process, which is still within the area of thought. Meditation is the freedom from thought...'

To cease thought is not an easy route, however: as Maxwell Cade says in *The Awakened Mind*, 'To learn to still the everyday mind, to stop the flow of idle chatter, the internal record player that perpetually that rolls on with ceaseless recriminations, rehearsals, puns, alliterations and even snatches of poetry and popular song, is the fundamental lesson of meditation.'

Arthur J. Deikman, in his *Deautomatization and The Mystic Experience* (further explored in *The Measure of Bliss*, p. 100), calls this category of inducement the 'trained-sensate', as opposed to the 'untrained-sensate' of spontaneous mystic experience: even if the result is the same or too similar to be easily distinguished, the difference is the deliberation. (The relative quality of the spontaneous and induced experience is discussed at the end of this chapter.)

Meditation is the basic means to all 'enlightenment', a state which, though fundamentally the same, is given a great variety of names in the East and in the West. In Yoga philosophy it is known as *samadhi* or *moksha*; in Zen Buddhism, *satori* or *kensho*; in Taoism, *the absolute Tao*; in Sufism, *fana*. That which Richard Bucke called *cosmic consciousness*, and St. Paul called *the peace that passeth all understanding*, Quakers call *the inner light*, Martin Buber the Jewish prophet, *the I-Thou relationship*, Carl Jung, *individuation*, and more recently Abraham Maslow, *peak experience*.

Much has been written on the use of drugs to facilitate mystic experience. Ever since the experimental work in the '60s with LSD (diethylamide of dilysergic acid), which was thought to provide a model for the study of schizophrenia, but was also found to trigger-off states closely resembling descriptions of mystic transport there has been widespread use of this substance (illegal, unless administered under medical supervision) to induce these extended 'realms of the unconscious'.

Other 'mind-opening' drugs that have a long history of use to induce mystical experience include many of plant origin, such as mescaline extracted from the *peyote* cactus and psilocybin from the *psilocybe* mushroom; both were used in this way in Mexico before and after the Spanish conquest. Whatever the drug, the end in view is the same: some form of chemical alteration of consciousness is applied to assist, prepare the way, and at some point to attain to mystic experience that may range from the spontaneous to a permanent state lived in the midst of ordinary life.

Apart from contemplative prayer, meditation and the use of drugs, there are, as outlined at the beginning of this section, many other ways of inducing mystical experience. These are examined in some detail by Dr Richard Petty in his contribution below (pp. 95-100).

The following contemporary or recent accounts – confined to the broadest categories – have all come as a result of some deliberate effort, whether mild or intense, of short or long practice.

Bliss Achieved with Aids

'The instruments of this investigation are a mind trained in
meditation, a sensitivity keyed up to the point of identifying
with that aspect of the one that is nonsolid, nonspatial,
timeless, effulgent, all-encompassing, the ability to conduct
consciousness beyond the point where it is the consciousness
of an "I" ' – Pir Vilayat Inayat Khan (Sufi Master)

Jacob Boehme, the 17th century mystic, recorded that he was once
suddenly transported into a state of bliss when his physical vision was
dazzled by sunlight reflected from a pewter plate. This light-induced
experience of the mystic may well find its explanation in terms of
modern neurology (dealt with later in the book), but it is an interesting
fact to note that it is not uncommon, and occurs both with and without
inducement, suggesting that it is a fundamental component of transcendence.

A related variation of this type of experience has been provided here
in a dramatic firsthand account by Theo Gimbel, at one time a prisoner
of first the Nazis and then the Red Army but today a practitioner of
alternative medicine, specialising in therapies involving light and colour.

A devout Christian
He describes what happened to him when the Red Army took over
from the Germans the camp in which he was imprisoned. In constant
despair and daily in fear of death, he continued to pray with calm
persistence. One night he was roughly awakened and taken from his
cell:

'I was shoved into a brilliantly lit room and with the guard pushing
his gun into my back stood there: far away on the other side of the
room, four officers were playing cards and drinking.

'I understood a little Russian by now and in the months since I had
been accused of being a spy, I had managed to learn a little more. After
some time, one looked up and said to the guard, "Who's this?" The
guard replied with my number and my name, but was waved off as he
obviously could not decipher much else.

'One of the officers fumbled amongst some papers on the table and
then attended to his game again. The light in the room seemed to have
got dimmer and dimmer. My eyes must have got used to it, but strangely
all the noise of laughing and argument over the game at the other side
of this world had also faded to a mere murmuring, like a small quiet
stream. There stood between this my place and the other place over

there a light which was not the reflection of any light issuing from the bulbs. I knew if there should be a power cut now, there would be no darkness. This cloud of light in the most unutterable peace remained for timeless moments.

'From far away came the voice of one of the men, "Go on, don't need him now!" And through the dawn we walked back to the camp. There was no breakfast, water with cabbage leaves and bread (one ounce) was already cancelled by the hut eldest, so I was told. But I was neither hungry nor tired.

'Weeks passed, I was several times on the list of transport "home", but whenever the list came back from the political office, my name was crossed out. At irregular intervals twice more I was rudely rushed to the gates, taken to this blaze of light, found the same wonder and peace, and was sent away again. I continued to pray unremittingly and to thank Christ for his protection and peace, and was sent away again.

'After one time, when we arrived again at the hut, the door was flung open and I was facing, at eye level, the 1,000 watt bulb again. The impact was so powerful that I had to tell myself, "stand still, show no emotion, let nothing be outwardly seen of any fear or uncertainty". But, indeed, under the circumstances, there was no fear or uncertainty – only this incredible peace, joy and absolute protection.

'This time, as I faced a new group of four officers playing cards, drinking vodka, laughing coarsely, as one of them turned to me to interrogate me, the now mellow, golden light suddenly divided itself into a shaft standing vertically between us and the officer suddenly made a waving gesture, indicating "forget it", and turned back to the game. Sounds had receded and all was so serene as I cannot remember ever feeling before.

'The same thing happened again, and this time as one of the officers stood up and began to move towards me, the golden light seemed to come between us, and the officer halted. He then returned to his table fumbled amongst some papers as if anxiously looking for a document, leaning eventually back in his chair, then indicating to the guard that I should be led away.

'At dawn, we came back to the camp, as usual now no food, but still this amazement of my return.

'Somehow the protection lasted, because I am able to write about this, but I have never forgotten – the light has been with me through the intervening years and gratitude.'

'A backcloth to life'

Experiences that are of a mystical or, at any rate, quasi-mystical, nature can be easily induced by the use of a hallucinogenic drug such as mescalin or LSD.

John Willmin has contributed a particularly lucid account of an experience of this type which, rather unusually for a drug experience, seems to have had permanent effects on his personality and outlook on life. This may have been because he was, in a sense, prepared for his experience of bliss by a previous concern with the spiritual aspects of life – he had read devotional literature of every variety, had attended a theological college and become a Baptist minister. Subsequently after a 'crisis of faith' followed by a nervous breakdown he had left the Church and was receiving psychotherapy involving the supervised use of LSD. He writes:

'. . . I was lying on a bed in a day hospital in a room alone, having had a dose of LSD. At first all sorts of intense feelings swept over me – Love, Anger, Fear, etc., in unbelievable strength. Then it happened. I lay still, with my eyes shut – and I experienced INTENSE AWARENESS. I *knew* I knew *everything*. I knew all the answers, because I had gone *beyond the questions*. The questions, reason, logic, were all irrelevant – I had gone beyond them. I knew this with absolute and utter conviction. Nothing mattered – life, pain, death – nothing mattered at all – except – AWARENESS. I knew *intuitively* that I had gone beyond all normal experience. I had transcended the dichotomies of good and evil, of material and immaterial, of past, present and future, of emotions, of personality. There were no more opposites. I was at a point beyond them *all*. I knew too that all things were *one* – and I was *part* of all things, and all things were part of *me*. I had transcended time, and religion and conceptions of "God". Everything just *IS*. It was *obvious* – it was satisfying to the nth degree.

'How long it lasted, I don't know – half an hour? Half a minute? Half a second? It didn't *matter*, *nothing* mattered.

'That is all I can say about it. The main characteristics were – (a) Utter certainty (b) Timelessness (c) Unity (d) "Obviousness" (e) "Satisfyingness" (f) Realisation that this was the *Ultimate* – that I had gone beyond everything else conceivable (g) Awareness (h) Completeness (i) Nothing mattered (j) "ISNESS".'

He described the long-term effects of the experience as follows:

'The realisation that IT is *there*. This has given a "back-cloth" to life. Whether it happens again or not, doesn't *matter* – it's *there* – nothing can change that. Fear of death has gone. Presumably at death we are absorbed into it ALL. Religious dogmas are puny and trivial. If they *help* people, so be it, but they are so inferior to REALITY that they are not worth bothering with. Difficulty of reconciling IT to everyday life. Slight disappointment that at the Ultimate there wasn't Personality – that there wasn't *God* – yet the ISNESS of Ultimate Reality was fully satisfying at all levels. Frustration at not being able to communicate it – except to the few who have experienced it. The realisation that, as IT is *there*, so it can be *partly* induced again by –

'(1) Meditation

'(2) Ceasing to conceptualise when looking at an object – just being aware of its ISNESS, especially trees, plants, and even artifacts. I have had minor experiences by looking at – dead leaves, my keys, Henry Moore's sculptures, trees, a pile of dirt, the curve in banisters, music, poetry, the folds in garments, a puddle, a dog's excreta, a stone, the light falling on a vase, shadows [Trigger-factors?].

'Sometimes I am more aware of it than at others. . . I am deeply grateful for it – it was the highlight of my life. I am 58, and it happened about 16 years ago, and it is still intensely real. I don't argue it, or try to explain it – arguments and explanations are irrelevant.'

Induction without intention

Vivien Gibson, a young widow, experienced a profoundly altered state of consciousness as an after-effect of taking, for therapeutic purposes, a large dose of insulin. Insulin is a substance naturally produced in the human pancreas, is present in the bodies of all living people, where it metabolises sugar, and is not normally regarded as an hallucinogen. Vivien Gibson's experience, as told by her, bears an uncanny resemblance to accounts of both drug-induced illuminations and spontaneous mystical states.

Vivien Gibson was emerging from her insulin coma when she experienced the following:

'It began with an overwhelming awareness that I understood *everything about everything*, and that the Universe wasn't complex at all, but beautifully, exquisitely, simple – although not, of course, describable in any terms that we know. I laughed with sheer joy at the absolute "rightness" of it. No doubt you know the jubilantly satisfying "click" one experiences when one finds the solution to, for instance, a complicated mathematical problem. Well, the experience I had was of a similar kind but carried to the ultimate. A king-size, super-hyper-Click!!! And with the feeling that I had "come home". It included the blissful awareness of unity, of being in all, all being in me. All this – I say "all" but really it was a single experience – merged into an intense and buoyant feeling of "Love": I felt as though I were breathing love and had love coursing through my veins; and this persisted for some time after regaining full consciousness. Every person I saw seemed to be very precious to me and I'd gladly have been of service to them in any way I could. It flashed into my mind that this, of course, was what is meant by "God is love", not "God is loving" or "God loves", but "GOD IS LOVE". (Not that I personally think in terms of "God", the nearest I can get is "Essence", essence which we block by concentration on *our* conception of "self".)

'I had no recollection of either reading or having any account of a mystical experience, although I have read a great deal since then. I am basically religious but totally unable to subscribe to any of the orthodox (or fringe) religions, which, even before my "M.E.", seemed to me to be somewhat parochial . . .

'I'd very much like to be able truthfully to say that this experience lastingly transformed my life, but alas . . . . it has been difficult to find the relevance of this past awareness of Ultimate Reality to everyday living. Nevertheless, I do, from time to time, find comfort in recalling this supreme moment of my life, and frequently wish I could experience it again. Sometimes when listening to music, or meditating, I feel on the very verge of losing myself again in the same rapture, but am too conscious of this fact and thus create a barrier.'

Meditation is the most widespread technique used for the induction of the mystical state. While meditation does not usually produce an 'instant bliss' of the sort associated with drug experience, its regular practice often eventually results in altered states of consciousness quite as spectacular as those induced by drugs.

Vanora Goodhart, a painter in oils, has contributed her graphic account of bliss attained through meditative techniques. She began by studying and then using the methods outlined in a book on Zen Buddhism written by Christmas Humphries – an author who combined dedication to Buddhism with being one of England's most distinguished judges.

She experienced a period of deep inner peace, felt 'radiantly happy inside', and came under the influence of a spiritual healer, Mrs Jean Meade, who encouraged her to continue meditating. Towards the end of 1977 she was sitting meditating when:

' . . .I felt a stirring at the base of my spine, and a slight pressure that rose up my back, at the same time a light began seeping through my closed eyelids, bright and gentle at first, but growing more and more intense. Frankly, I have a very analytical mind and I immediately tried to rationalise what was happening. Momentarily, I opened my eyes to make sure this Light was not coming from anywhere in the room – it was most certainly not.'

'A great rush of power'

'I closed my eyes again. The intensity grew and grew. If my eyes had been open I should have felt it was blinding. Moreover, there was a great power and strength in this Light, that was by now burning wonderfully deep into my emotions. The bliss was so totally overwhelming, that the still rationalizing part of me wondered whether I could bear it – was I dying, was I leaving my body? The pins and needles that started in my head were now spreading down through my body, at the same time I felt I was being drawn upwards and in a great and wonderful rush of power that rose eventually to a crescendo and bathed me through and through with glorious burning, embracing Light. Then slowly, gently, I came back, again there was the powerful feeling of being drawn, this time back down into my body. During this time I had at one point flung my arms open as if I wanted to open my heart physically to the Light.

Now I felt I was back, the Light was still glowing gently, but I knew I should open my eyes. I realized I was literally drenched in perspiration and my heart was beating hard.

'Immediately I called my mother, desperate to convey at once my experience. I blurted out the strange statement "it's all true", referring not directly to what had happened to me, but as a confirmation of the fact that we must never, never doubt the reality of our souls or of the truth and power of the Spirit, because now I *knew*. By this time the tears of joy were streaming down my face.

'It is interesting to note that at this time in my life, I had absolutely no knowledge from any source of what a mystical experience can be like, therefore I was frankly in a state of ecstatic shock.

'Incidentally, I looked at my watch when I "came back" and saw that the experience had lasted 20 minutes, though to me it could have been a couple of minutes or a couple of hours, as I had no awareness of physical time while this was happening.

'As a short conclusion to all this I would just like to say, that my life from that time to the present day has been in a worldly or physical sense immeasurably changed for the better and that my life in the spiritual sense has been, and is, dedicated to the reality of the Great Spirit behind all physical manifestation, and my ambition is always to know and be used more by the power of Light or Love.'

It may well be significant that Vanora Goodhart's experience began with what she calls a stirring at the base of her spine. For in yogic theory this area is associated with 'Kundalini' – a psychic powerhouse which in its latent form is symbolised as a coiled serpent 'sleeping' at the base of the spine.

The arousal of this 'serpent', and the consequent achievement of bliss, is the object of Kundalini Yoga. The process has been described in detail by many of the devotees of this technique. Before quoting one of these it is necessary to give a brief description of the theoretical basis, which could well be called 'mystical anatomy', underlying Kundalini Yoga.

It is conceived that associated with, but not part of, the physical body are a number of centres of physical energy, called *chakras* or *padmas*. Each of these centres is symbolised as a lotus with a varying number of petals, the highest being the 'thousand petalled lotus' which is associated with the brain and is 'the abode of Siva', the seat of 'Consciousness-Bliss'. The practitioner of Kundalini Yoga aims to arouse the sleeping serpent-power and to transmit its energy upwards through subtle pathways associated with the spine, thus successively vivifying each of the *chakras*. Just how dramatic the effects of such an arousal of the Kundalini can be is made apparent in the following account, extracted from Gopi Krishna's *Kundalini – the evolutionary energy in man* (1971):

'. . .I sat breathing slowly and rhythmically, my attention drawn towards the crown of my head, contemplating an imaginary lotus in full bloom, radiating light.

'I sat steadily, unmoving and erect, my thoughts uninterruptedly centred on the shining lotus, intent on keeping my attention from wandering and bringing it back again and again whenever it moved in any other direction. The intensity of concentration interrupted my breathing; gradually it slowed down to such an extent that at times it was barely perceptible. My whole being was so engrossed in the contemplation of the lotus that for several minutes at a time I lost touch with my body and surroundings. During such intervals I used to feel as if I were poised in mid-air, without any feeling of a body around me. The only object of which I was aware was a lotus of brilliant colour, emitting rays of light. This experience has happened to many people who practice meditation in any form regularly for a sufficient length of time, but what followed on that fateful morning in my case, changing the whole course of my life and outlook, has happened to few.

'During one such spell of intense concentration I suddenly felt a strange sensation below the base of the spine, at the place touching the seat, while I sat cross-legged on a folded blanket spread on the floor. The sensation was so extraordinary and so pleasing that my attention was unexpectedly withdrawn from the point on which it was focused, the sensation ceased. Thinking it to be a trick played by my imagination to relax the tension, I dismissed the matter from my mind and brought my attention back to the point from which it had wandered. Again I fixed it on the lotus, and as the image grew clear and distinct at the top of my head, again the sensation occurred. This time I tried to maintain the fixity of my attention and succeeded for a few seconds, but the sensation extending upwards grew so intense and was so extraordinary, as compared to anything I had experienced before, that in spite of myself my mind went towards it, and at that very moment it again disappeared. I was now convinced that something unusual had happened for which my daily practice of concentration was probably responsible.'

'A roar like that of a waterfall'
'I had read glowing accounts, written by learned men, of great benefits resulting from concentration and of miraculous powers acquired by yogis through such exercises. My heart began to beat wildly, and I found it difficult to bring my attention to the required degree of fixity. After a while I grew composed and was soon as deep in meditation as before. When completely immersed I again experienced the sensation, but this time, instead of allowing my mind to leave the point where I had fixed it, I maintained a rigidity of attention throughout. The sensation again extended upwards, growing in intensity, and I felt myself wavering; but with a great effort I kept my attention centred round the lotus. Suddenly, with a roar like that of a waterfall, I felt a stream of liquid light entering my brain through the spinal cord.

'Entirely unprepared for such a development, I was completely taken by surprise; but regaining self-control instantaneously, I remained sitting in the same posture, keeping my mind on the point of concentration. The illumination grew brighter and brighter, the roaring louder, I experienced a rocking sensation and then felt myself slipping out of my body, entirely enveloped in a halo of light. It grew wider and wider, spreading outward while the body, normally the immediate object of its perception, appeared to have receded into the distance until I became entirely unconscious of it. I was now all consciousness, without any outline, without any idea of a corporeal appendage, without any feeling or sensation coming from the senses, immersed in a sea of light simultaneously conscious and aware of every point, spread out, as it were, in all directions without any barrier or material obstruction.

I was no longer myself, or to be more accurate, no longer as I knew myself to be, a small point of awareness confined in a body, but instead was a vast circle of consciousness in which the body was but a point, bathed in light and in a state of exaltation and happiness impossible to describe.

'After some time, the duration of which I could not judge, the circle began to narrow down; I felt myself contracting, becoming smaller and smaller, until I became dimly conscious of the outline of my body, then more clearly; and as I slipped back to my old condition, I became suddenly aware of the noises in the street, felt again my arms and legs and head, and once more became my narrow self in touch with body and surroundings. When I opened my eyes and looked about, I felt a little dazed and bewildered, as if coming back from a strange land completely foreign to me. The sun had risen and was shining full on my face, warm and soothing . . . .

'What had happened to me? Was I the victim of a hallucination? Or had I by some strange vagary of fate succeeded in experiencing the Transcendental? Had I really succeeded where millions of others had failed? Was there, after all, really some truth in the oft-repeated claim of the sages and ascetics of India, made for thousands of years and verified and repeated generation after generation, that it was possible to apprehend reality in this life if one followed certain rules of conduct and practised meditation in a certain way? . . . . Had I been lucky enough to find the key to this wonderful mechanism [kundalini], which was wrapped up in the legendary mist of ages, about which people talked and whispered without having seen it in action in themselves or in others?

' . . . Could it be that in my condition of extreme concentration I had mistaken it [the sun] for the effulgent halo that had surrounded me in the superconscious state? I closed my eyes again, allowing the rays of the sun to play upon my face. No, the glow that I could perceive across my closed eyelids was quite different. It was external and had not that splendour. The light I had experienced was internal, an integral part of enlarged consciousness, a part of my self.'

Feeling very strange indeed, Gopi Krishna did not mention this experience to his wife, and left for work as usual – but his mind reverted again and again to the experience. After unsuccessful attempts to repeat the experience, he finally managed to steady his wandering thoughts and achieve the same fixity of attention on the crown of the head, visualising a lotus in full bloom as was his custom, and experienced again the upward-moving current. Again, there was the rush and roaring noise, the stream of effulgent light that seemed to enter his brain, filling him with 'power and vitality'. He felt himself expanding in all directions, spreading beyond the boundaries of flesh, entirely absorbed in the contemplation of a brilliant conscious glow, one with it and yet not entirely merged in it.

The condition lasted a shorter time than the previous experience and the feeling of exaltation was not so strong, yet as time went on he felt that he lived suspended by a thread, 'swinging between . . . sanity and insanity, between light and darkness, heaven and earth.'

He had meditated since he was 17, attempted self-mastery of what he felt were his weaknesses and failures, studied the *Bhagavad Gita* in an effort to resolve the conflict between his material and spiritual aims, but now he had been roused beyond division, he lived in both worlds at once. 'One,' he wrote later, 'is the sensory world which we all share together – the world of sight, touch, smell, taste and sound – the other is an amazing supersensory world, which to the best of my knowledge, I share alone, or perhaps, with extremely few others unknown to me . . . . I am always conscious of a luminous glow not only in my interior, but pervading the whole field of my vision during the hours of my wakefulness. I literally live in a world of light. It is, as it were, a light filling me with a lustre so beautiful and ravishing that my attention is again and again drawn towards it. In fact, it is the normal state of my perception now. Light, both within and without, and a distinct music in my ears, are the two prominent features of my transformed being. It is as if, in my interior, I live in a charming, radiant and melodious world. A sense of its fascination is always present in me. The harmony is disturbed, more or less, in unhealthy states of the body in the same way as sickness disturbs the poise of the normal mind. This disturbance is only occasional. Normally an indwelling joy and harmony make my life much more happy and serene than it was before my transformation.'

Gopi Krishna's experience affected not only his inner but his outer life – he was led to found the Research Institute for Kundalini and to make exhaustive efforts to interest scientists in Kundalini Yoga.

The sort of 'sudden breakthrough' experienced by Gopi Krishna is sometimes deliberately induced by the action of a yogic Guru (teacher). In his autobiography Paramhansa Yogananda, who lived in the West for over 30 years and was responsible for introducing many thousands to Yogic theory and technique, writes lucidly of such a Guru-induced breakthrough. His Master called him, told him that his 'heart's desire should be fulfilled' and struck him gently on the chest.

'An oceanic joy, a sea of mirth'

'My body became immovably rooted; breath was drawn out of my lungs as if by some huge magnet. Soul and mind instantly lost their physical bondage, and streamed out like a fluid piercing light from my every pore. The flesh was as though dead, yet in my intense awareness I knew that never before had I been fully alive. My sense of identity was no longer narrowly confined to a body, but embraced the circumambient atoms. People on distant streets seemed to be moving gently over my own remote periphery. The roots of plants and trees appeared through a dim transparency of the soil; I discerned the inward flow of their sap.

'The whole vicinity lay bare before me. My ordinary frontal vision was now changed to a vast spherical sight, simultaneously all-perceptive. Through the back of my head I saw men strolling far down Rai Ghat Lane, and noticed also a white cow who was leisurely approaching. When she reached the space in front of the open ashram gate, I observed her as though with my physical eyes. As she passed by, behind the brick wall, I saw her clearly still.

'All objects within my panoramic gaze trembled and vibrated like quick motion pictures . . . The unifying light alternated with material-isations of form, the metamorphoses revealing the law of cause and effect in creation.

'An oceanic joy broke upon calm endless shores of my soul. The Spirit of God, I realised, is exhaustless Bliss; His body is countless tissues of light. A swelling glory within me began to envelop towns, continents, the earth, solar and stellar systems, tenuous nebulae, and floating universes. The entire cosmos, gently luminous, like a city seen afar at night, glimmered within the infinitude of my being. The dazzling light beyond the sharply etched global outlines faded somewhat at the farthest edges; there I could see a mellow radiance, ever-undiminished. It was inde-scribably subtle; the planetary pictures were formed of a grosser light . . .

'I recognised the centre of the empyrean as a point of intuitive perception in my heart. Irradiating splendour issued from my nucleus to every part of the universal structure. Blissful *amrita*, the nectar of immortality, pulsed through me with a quicksilverlike fluidity. The creative voice of God I heard resounding as *Aum**, the vibration of the Cosmic Motor.

'Suddenly the breath returned to my lungs. With a disappointment almost unbearable, I realised that my infinite immensity was lost. Once more I was limited to the humiliating cage of a body, not easily accommo-

---

* 'In the beginning was the Word (*Logos*) and the Word was with God, and the Word was God' (the opening words of St John's Gospel).

dative to the Spirit. Like a prodigal child, I had run away from my macrocosmic home and imprisoned myself in a paltry microcosm.

'My guru was standing motionless before me; I started to drop at his holy feet in gratitude for the experience in cosmic consciousness which I had long passionately sought. He held me upright, and spoke calmly, unpretentiously

' "You must not get overdrunk with ecstasy. Much work yet remains for you in the world. Come, let us sweep the balcony floor; then we shall walk by the Ganges."

'I fetched a broom; Master, I knew, was teaching me the secret of balanced living. The soul must stretch over the cosmogonic abysses, while the body performs its daily duties. I saw our bodies as two astral pictures, moving over a road by the river whose essence was sheer light.

' "It is the Spirit of God that actively sustains every form and force in the universe; yet He is transcendental and aloof in the blissful uncreated void beyond the worlds of vibratory phenomena," Master explained. "Saints who realise their divinity even while in the flesh know a similar twofold existence. Consciously engaging in earthly work, they yet remain immersed in an inward beatitude.

' "The Lord has created all men from the limitless joy of His being. Though they are painfully cramped by the body, God knows that souls made in His image shall ultimately rise above all sense identifications and reunite with Him."

'The cosmic vision left many permanent lessons. By daily stilling my thoughts, I could win release from the delusive conviction that my body was a mass of flesh and bones, traversing the hard soil of matter. The breath and the restless mind, I saw, are like storms which lash the ocean of light into waves of material forms – earth, sky, human beings, animals, birds, trees. No perception of the Infinite as One Light can be had except by calming those storms. As often as I silence the two natural tumults, I beheld the multitudinous waves of creation melt into one lucent sea, even as the waves of the ocean, their tempests subsiding, serenely dissolve into unity.

'A master bestows the divine experience of cosmic consciousness when his disciple, by meditation, has strengthened his mind to a degree where the vast vistas would not overwhelm him. The experience can never be given through one's mere intellectual willingness or open-mindedness. Only adequate enlargement by yoga practice and devotional bhakti (worship) can prepare the mind to absorb the liberating shock of omnipresence. It comes with a natural inevitability to the sincere devotee. His intense craving begins to pull at God with an irresistible force.

The Lord, as the Cosmic Vision, is drawn by the seeker's magnetic ardour into his range of consciousness.'

In his later years Paramhansa Yogananda wrote a poem entitled *Samadhi*, of which the last verse reads:

Gone forever, fitful, flickering shadows of
        mortal memory.
Spotless is my mental sky, below, ahead, and
        high above.
Eternity and I, one united ray.
A tiny bubble of laughter, I
Am become the Sea of Mirth Itself.'

The 'Sea of Mirth' of the last line is particularly interesting. For laughter seems to feature in many mystic experiences, and almost all Eastern mystics, with their easy, bubbling-over of merriment, which appears to be a corollary of mastery and advancement (often misunderstood in the West as 'foolish' giggling), find their perspective of wholeness leading to humour in the transient.

Peter Russell, scientist, author of *The Awakening Earth* and teacher of Transcendental Meditation, tells of a mystic experience, which involved what some have called 'the mystic joke'.

'Dancing for joy'

'I had been sitting in a long and peaceful meditation. Or at least, most of it was peaceful, the initial stages had been preoccupied with a personal problem as to whether I should do one of two things. Otherwise there was nothing extraordinary about the meditation, except perhaps it was very still and more peaceful than usual. Afterwards I laid down on the floor for a few minutes, as is my normal practice. Suddenly, for no apparent reason, waves of bliss and happiness started moving through my body. It was very much a physical sensation which seemed to come somewhere in the centre of the chest.

'As they spread through my body I felt ridiculously happy, so much so that my inner smiles broke out into spontaneous laughter. I lay there laughing and laughing until suddenly the problem I had been immersed in flitted through my mind. It now seemed silly and insignificant; and anyway, either solution would be fine. The fact that I could have become so immersed in it just made me laugh more and more.

'Then my body started a dancing movement, if you can call it that. Lying on the floor the whole body began a series of movements rather reminiscent of Indian dancing. Arms, legs, hands, body, neck all flowing, waving and rippling completely spontaneously. This lasted for about ten minutes, gradually subsiding and leaving me in a state of incredible peace and well-being.

'Coming out into the garden the whole world seemed fresher and crisper, and much more immediate. The most interesting thing was that the problem I had been so pre-occupied with remained far away and insignificant – and in fact it has never bothered me since.'

Naturally, the foregoing is only a small sampling of the millions of experiences stretched out across the globe, and of the myriad techniques for inducing them: but these are sufficient to provide the basis for further exploration.

The Relative Merits of the Spontaneous and Induced Experiences

'. . .experiences which seem remote from each other in the individual are perhaps all equally near in the universal' – Edward Carpenter, *From Adam's Peak to Elephanta* (1892)

It is likely that the fundamental differences, if any, between an experience that comes as 'gratuitous grace', without preparation or expectation, and one that comes as a result of some form or another of effort or inducement, will never be discerned or defined with absolute finality. If they are, it will be because the gap between the experiential and the experimental has been bridged by some as-yet-to-be-uncovered mode of perception.

The value of drug-induced experience
In the meantime, as a contribution towards that mode, there is both the conviction of those who have experienced the spontaneous that it could not possibly be equalled in quality by the induced, and the equally strong conviction of those who have had induced experience that it was, beyond hair-splitting or debate, 'the ultimate experience'.

Aldous Huxley, in his book *Heaven and Hell* (1956) wrote:

'. . .'Exponents of a Nothing-But philosophy will answer that, since changes in body chemistry can create the conditions favourable to visionary and mystical experience, visionary and mystical experiences cannot be what they claim to be, what for those who had had them, they self-evidently are. But this, of course, is a *non sequitur*. A similar conclusion will be reached by those whose philosophy is unduly 'spiritual'.

God, they will insist, is a spirit and is to be worshipped in spirit. Therefore an experience which is chemically conditioned cannot be an experience of the divine. But, in one way or another, *all* our experiences are chemically conditioned, and if we imagine that some of them are purely 'spiritual', purely 'intellectal', purely 'aesthetic', it is merely because we have never troubled to investigate the internal chemical environment at the moment of their occurrence.

'Furthermore, it is a matter of historical record that most contemplatives worked systematically to modify their body chemistry, with a view to creating the internal conditions favourable to a spiritual insight. When they were not starving themselves into low blood sugar and vitamin deficiency, they were beating themselves into intoxication by histamine, adrenalin and decomposed protein in uncomfortable positions in order to create the psycho-physical symptoms of stress.

'In the intervals they sang interminable psalms, thus increasing the amount of carbon dioxide in the lungs and the blood stream, or, if they were Orientals, they did breathing exercises to accomplish the same purpose.

'Today we know how to lower the efficiency of the cerebral reducing valve by direct chemical action, and without the risk of inflicting serious damage on the psycho-physical organism. For an aspiring mystic to revert, in the present state of knowledge, to prolonged fasting and violent self-flagellation would be as senseless as it would be for an aspiring cook to behave like Charles Lamb's Chinaman, who burned down the house in order to roast a pig.

'Knowing as he does (or at least as he can know, if he so desires) what are the chemical conditions of transcendental experience, the aspiring mystic should turn for technical help to the specialists – in pharmacology, in biochemistry, in physiology and neurology, in psychology and psychiatry, and parapsychology. And on their part, of course, the specialists should turn, out of their respective pigeonholes, to the artist, the sibyl, the visionary, the mystic – all those, in a word, who have had experience of the Other World, and who know, in their different ways, what to do with that experience.'

While his experiments with LSD and mescalin were in the spirit of research, and relatively few, Aldous Húxley wrote of them so articulately in his immaculate and imaginative prose that untold thousands of people have been influenced, had their minds opened to the fine points of drug-induced experience (though he made a firm differentiation between visionary and mystic experience, stating that the former was not by definition necessarily a mystic experience). He, himself, believed drug experience could be equated with the heights of spontaneous experience, and saw their usefulness in expanding the general consciousness of mankind.

Professor R.C. Zaehner, in his book *Mysticism: Sacred and Profane* (1957), did not agree, and took issue with this view. He felt that there was no comparison between 'religious' or 'sacred' mystic experience and that induced by using drugs. He had had some very unpleasant experiences under drugs, and he pointed out that alcohol, as well as the long-used Indian hemp (hashish), has produced spurious ecstasies which can only be forms of escape wherein the human ego stands outside itself, and which are not to be associated with the acknowledged illuminations of the saints!

On the other hand, he seems not to have recognised the effects of their ascetic practices on the nervous system of those saints, which might have altered their states of consciousness in ways imperceptibly different to those induced by drugs.

Some people believe that one distinct difference between the spontaneous and drug-induced experience is in the quality of the after-effect. The majority of those who have the 'grand' spontaneous experience are profoundly uplifted for the rest of their lives, many becoming deeply religious, and the claim is made that drug-induced experience does not necessarily have this effect, even though it is equally overwhelming. It is said that it must always be induced again, and Dr Sidney Cohen, in *The Drugs of Hallucination* has said, 'A pill does not construct character, educate the emotions, or improve the intelligence. It is not a spiritual labour-saving device, salvation, instant wisdom, or short cut to maturity.'

Nevertheless, there is no substantial support for this. The mystic experiences of some, as reported in various works of research dealing with LSD and other drugs seem to indicate equally profound changes toward a more compassionate view of life, higher aspirations and a spiritual or religious confirmation or re-orientation. Unless there were some way to analyse, dissect, perhaps compute, even the subtlest aspect of each type of experience, every image, colour, sound, smell, feeling, alteration of reality and all sorts of other factors, comparisons must inevitably vanish into the thin air of 'I can't explain. I just know'. After all, one can never totally share another person's experience as at first hand.

A firm effort to investigate the similarities between the two types of experience was made in the '60s by Walter N. Pahnke, Director of Clinical Sciences Research at the Maryland State Psychiatric Research Center in Baltimore, Maryland (USA). In an experimental examination of the claim that psychedelic drug experience could resemble mystic experience, 'because of the frequency with which some of the subjects who have experimented with synthesized mescaline, LSD, or psilocybin have used mystical and religious language to describe their experiences,' an empirical study was designed to investigate in a systematic and scientific way the similarities and differences between the two kinds of experiences.

First, a 'phenomenological typology' of the mystical state was carefully defined, using that of William James, the distinguished American psychologist, as a guide. Then some drug experiences were studied by conducting a 'double-blind' controlled experiment with subjects whose religious background and experience, as well as personality, had been measured *before* their drug experiences. Preparation of the subject, the setting under which the drug was administered, and the collection of data were made as uniform as possible.

The nine-category typology of the mystic state was used as a basis for measurement of the psychedelic drug experiences. The work of W.T. Stace was consulted and his categories for the mystic state (see Introduction) used.

'The purpose of the experiment in which psilocybin was administered in a religious context was to gather empirical data about the state of consciousness experienced. In a private chapel on Good Friday, 20 Christian theological students, 10 of whom had been given psilocybin one and one-half hours earlier, listened over loudspeakers to a two-and-one-half-hour religious service which was in actual progress in another part of the building and which consisted of organ music, four solos, readings, prayers, and personal meditation.'

The idea was to create an atmosphere broadly comparable to that achieved by tribes using natural drug substances in religious ceremonies. In the weeks before the experiment there was a five-hour preparation and screening procedure for each participant, which included psychological tests, medical history, physical examination, questionnaires on religious attitudes and experiences, interviews and group interaction.

All 20 subjects were graduate student volunteers, of middle class, Protestant backgrounds, one from a denominational seminary in the free-church tradition. None had prior experience with drugs. Relaxation and friendship within the group was encouraged and no mention was made of the typology of the mystic state. In the double-blind approach no one employed in the experiment, nor any of the participants, knew the specific contents of the outwardly identical capsules which were administered.

Half of the subjects received psilocybin, and without prior knowledge of the effects, the other 10 subjects each received 200 mg of nicotinic acid, a vitamin which causes *transient* feelings of warmth and tingling of the skin.

On the experimental day, tape recordings were made both of individual reactions immediately after the religious service, and of the group discussions which followed. Each subject wrote an immediate account of his experience, and within the week all subjects had turned in a 147-item questionnaire designed to appraise the various phenomena of the typology, quantitatively and qualitatively.

This formed the basis of a subsequent interview lasting an hour and a half, which was tape-recorded, and six months later every subject was interviewed again with a follow-up, three-part questionnaire, which was then organised into two Tables of Percentage scores based on the typology, delineating the various differences between the Experimental versus the Control Group.

Without going into the specific details of differences between the two groups, which are considerable, the overall findings which emerged were that 'the subjects who were given psilocybin found the religious service more meaningful, both at the time and later, than did the control subjects. This finding raises the possibility that psychedelic drug experiences in a religious setting may be able to illuminate the dynamics and significance of worship.

'. . . . Although our experimental results indicated predominantly positive and beneficial subjective effects, possible dangers must not be underestimated and should be thoroughly evaluated by specific research designed to discover the causes and methods of prevention of physical or psychological harm, both short-term and long-term . . .': not only dependence but 'The intense subjective pleasure and enjoyment of the experience for its own sake could lead to escapism and withdrawal from the world . . . .

'A better scientific understanding of the mechanisms and application of mysticism has the potential for a greater appreciation and respect for heretofore rarely explored areas of human consciousness. If these areas have relevance for man's spiritual life, this should be a cause of rejoicing, not alarm. If the values nurtured by religion are fundamental for an understanding of the nature of man, then careful and sensitive scientific research into the experimental side of man's existence has the potential for illumination of these values.

One point that needs to be made here, is that, as Walter N. Pahnke himself states: 'Although a drug experience might seem "unearned" when compared with the rigorous discipline which many mystics describe as necessary, our evidence has suggested that' despite careful preparation 'positive mystical experience with psychedelic drugs is by no means automatic.'

In other words, the drug itself may be the trigger-factor, in which it is 'a necessary but not sufficient condition . . .' The hardest work may come after the experience, in the effort to integrate the experience with everyday life.

Conversely, while 'many persons may not need the drug-facilitated mystical experience, there are others who would never be aware of the undeveloped potential within themselves, or be inspired to work in this direction without such an experience.' Gratuitous grace, therefore, may come as a gift earned and deserved, or not earned and not particularly deserved.

TM and mystical states

Probably the most widely-applied method of inducing mystic experience today is that of Transcendental Meditation (TM). Brought to the West in 1958 by His Holiness Maharishi Maheshi Yogi, a physics graduate of Allahabad University and meditation teacher in India, this method of reaching 'Cosmic Consciousness' has in its directness and simplicity of technique, almost eliminated the awkwardness felt by Westerners for Eastern spiritual systems aiming for Bliss. More than the *nature* of God, TM emphasises the importance of deep relaxation; of 'harmonising' the nervous system by bringing it to 'the point of least excitation' wherein thought dies away and higher levels of consciousness are experienced. Its growth was vastly accelerated by work carried out by R.K. Wallace and Herbert Benson in 1970 at the Harvard Medical School. They conducted studies that showed the physiological correlates of TM. These included decrease in oxygen consumption; reductions in carbon dioxide elimination, heart and respiratory rate, in blood pressure, blood lactate, muscle tone and blood cortisone levels; increase in apparent basal skin resistance (which can be used as an accurate measure of the extent of relaxation), and changes in the pattern of brain electrical activity (brain waves), illustrating altogether an 'alert, hypometabolic state' (a restful state brought about by decreased activity of the sympathetic nervous system).

With this scientific validation, TM became 'respectable', could be approached with no greater ambitions in mind than increased energy and good health, less irritability, increased creativity, reduction of every kind of stress and tension and a calmer, more positive outlook on life in general. What did not need to be mentioned was that with these conditions the consciousness was insidiously led to higher ambitions, to interest in, and desire for, ascending levels of a hierarchy climaxed by the ultimate mystic experience of 'God-Consciousness'. In this context, there is little difference between TM and other systems such as Zazen (the meditation of Zen, meaning 'just sitting'); the Yogic meditations of Patanjali (concentrating upon one particular idea or object unwaveringly); Buddhist ('Mindfulness' of breathing, similiar to Zen method); but this fact has not emerged sufficiently to stay the immense Western infiltration of TM.

Transcendental Meditation now has a following in excess of one million in all professions, businesses, and walks of life, including the government in the USA, has centres in over 60 countries, a World Plan for 3,600 centres world-wide; a centre for scientific research in Switzerland and a University in Iowa. The Maharishi has now inaugurated his 'Age of Enlightenment', based on a new statistical proposition (arrived at through controlled experiments with segments of the populations of towns and cities) that when 1 per cent of the world's population practises transcendental meditation fifteen minutes twice daily, the result will be a global 'phase transition' from chaos and confusion to order and peace.

This is not by any means a full run-down on the extent of the TM organisation, just a sketch to show the scope, to say nothing of the potential, of sought cosmic consciousness. Is TM experience superior to the drugs it so often replaces? Is spontaneous experience superior to TM? To drugs? To any form of induction? Possible answers to these and other questions which have been raised at an earlier stage are considered in the second half of this book.

5
A Spectrum of Original Theories About Bliss

'The immeasurable is the primary and independent source of all reality. . . . Measure is a secondary and dependent aspect of this reality' – David Bohm, *Wholeness and the Implicate Order* (1980)

Having outlined the history of mystic experience, presented an overview of current statistical surveys of its occurrence, then roughly divided it into two main categories, spontaneous and induced, this exploration is now opened to a free range of hypothesis, personal observation and opinion, much of it specially contributed, the rest quoted from recent works on the subject.

The general classification of the theories or viewpoints presented here are those largely concerned with psychology, psychotherapy, medicine, neurophysiology (embracing epilepsy and schizophrenia), biofeedback, biology, physics, theology, ecology, clinical 'death' and philosophy.

These subjects, of course, are examined only for their relevance to ideas about mystic experience of the bliss variety. Some of the material presented is specific and technical, some is more intuitively expressed, outlining concepts based on an experiential feeling of 'knowledge'. Some contributions are quite short, some lengthy. It has seemed best to leave this unevenness rather than to tailor every entry for the sake of uniformity of presentation.

The order of the spectrum is not precise for the reason that the subject-matter is not entirely separable, with one category often sliding into that of another, and some repetition and overlapping is inevitable.

There must be many thousands of speculative theories and beliefs on the nature of what actually takes place in a mystic experience, and no doubt several volumes would be needed to contain them, but these given here are at least a start, at most a first stage of an immense, perhaps illimitable, journey of discovery.

Bliss, Medicine, Psychology and Neurophysiology

'A conscious universe is the only reality which can include
human consciousness. Only a conscious universe is relevant
to the whole of human life . . .' – Jacob Needleman, *A Sense
of the Cosmos*

An increasing number of medical practitioners are showing an interest
in all that lies beyond the known borders of physical science, as well as
in psychosomatic medicine.

One such is Dr Jonathon Meads, a General Practitioner of Taunton,
Somerset, who has himself experienced moments of 'great peace and
oneness with everything round me, of the falling away of all cares, of an
emotional need to dedicate my life to this Energy that flows in, around
and through me'. Dr Meads has taken a degree in Transpersonal
Psychology, partly in order to understand and relate better to the inner
needs of his patients. He takes the view that if they feel they can tell him
anything and not be considered 'mad', and that he is as 'mad' as they
are, then mystic experience often comes out in the open, with benefit to
both therapy and research.

Asked what he thought took place in what he called 'States of Bliss', he
wrote:

'I believe that flowing and through everything – i.e., in the "vast"
inter-atomic particle space, is the Life Force, Holy Spirit; some form of
energy. This keeps every cell of man alive. This energy enters the body
through the Pineal and Pituitary glands. There are intimate connections
between these glands and the other endocrine glands and the central
nervous system.

'If something turns man's consciousness fully away from all the
distractions round, his conscious mind can respond and enhance this
energy flow. It is as if the spirit within can respond to the spirit without.

'I feel that as man has now made his life easier through his technology;
that in general his health is better and that he is having more free time,
slowly he will come to find the exploration of his inner and spiritual
worlds as exciting as he has found the exploration of the physical
world.'

In answer to the specific question: What is the correlation between
the non-induced and drug-induced bliss experience? Stanley Krippner,
speaking from the psychological viewpoint, made an interesting point
that all mystical experiences may well be found to have psychophysical
correlates but that there is no reason to suppose that they will be
reducible to physical phenomena – and that even if they were, this

would not invalidate them. Stanley Krippner, who teaches at the Humanistic Psychology Institute, San Francisco and is known for work on *Dream Telepathy*, speculates thus:

'In my opinion, there is no essential difference between these two types of mystic experiences. I would hold that the drugs are acting as catalysts and that the psyche is doing essential work. The "Good Friday" experiment by Walter Pahnke [see previous chapter] demonstrated that drug-induced mystic experience closely paralleled the descriptions of non-drug counterparts.

'Over the centuries, experiences with *peyote* and *psylocibe* mushrooms have provided their users with mystic experiences. Pahnke drew upon the writings of W.T. Stace in delineating the characteristics of mystic experience (e.g., unity, transcendence, ineffability, peace, bliss...[to which] I would add another: *transformation.* I would hold that if a mystic experience does not change a person's life (attitudes, beliefs, behaviour, etc.) it is a lesser experience mystically than one which does transform.

'Because drug-induced experiences might be triggered prematurely (before an individual is ready for them), it is possible that they may, as a group, rate lower on this dimension. However, we really do not know if this is the case....

'True, there are hazards of drug use (but only in "civilised" cultures; primitive people appear to have had no serious problem with peyote, mushrooms, etc.). But there are also hazards in meditation, fasting, sensory deprivation, and other practices associated with mystic experience. Gope Krishna's initial kundalini experience is an eloquent testimony to the dangers of an unprepared person attempting to "force" mysticism. Spontaneous mystic experience is basically without hazard – unless the experiencer lives in a culture in which these experiences are regarded as symptoms of mental illness by those consulted after the episode occurs.

'My own opinion of mystic experience is that it is characterised by the dimensions cited above (and others to be found in Pahnke's listing). The essential element to me, is a union of the experiencer with God, the cosmos, the Tao, divine energy, or whatever he or she chooses to call what is "greater than the self". This is distinguished from religious experience which is an encounter of the individual with God, the Ground of Being, etc. Religious experience may be equally transforming. I feel the different cultures favor one experience or the other, with Eastern thought more likely to produce mystic experience and Western thought more likely to produce religious experience....

'I suspect that mystic experiences will be found to have psycho-physiological correlates, but that they will not be found to be reducible to physical phenomena. Yet even if they were, this would not make them any the less valuable and important.

'Summing up, I would say that: In mystic experience, one unites with the "beyond". In religious experience, one might meet the "beyond", and even dialogue with the "beyond", but one would not lose one's sense of self during the experience.'

Stanley Krippner, who wished to undergo drug-induced mystical experience firsthand, took part in an experiment conducted by Dr Timothy Leary, the Harvard academic who went on to become the world's best known advocate of illumination-through-drugs. Subsequently he wrote an exceptionally clear description, entitled *Music to Eat Mushrooms By*, of his personal experience of the effects of psilocybin, an alkaloid derived from a variety of mushroom used in some Amerindian religious rites.

He began by experiencing the seemingly heightened perceptions associated with the use of most hallucinogenic substances. Thus, for example, an apple tasted like 'the food of the gods', vanilla essence smelled 'delectable', and he heard music 'as he had never heard it before'. Even more remarkable were his visual impressions, his surroundings seemingly transformed into a vision of beauty and his fellow experimenters – three graduate psychology students – becoming 'positively radiant', their bodies 'vibrant and glowing'. His sense of time and place altered:

'. . .I experienced a complete negation of time as I had previously conceived it. I felt as if I could travel in the past, present, or future.

'At one moment, I was in the court of Kubla Khan, admiring the rich brocades of the emperor's gown and noting the fine detailed embroidery of his courtiers' cloaks.

'The next moment I was in a future utopia at a concert being held in an immense auditorium. The walls were violet and silver, the architecture resembled Eero Saarinen's wildest geometric formulations, the orchestra glistened in its brilliantly ostentatious costumery.

'Within an instant I was at the court of Versailles with Benjamin Franklin. The great old sage was more impressive in his wisdom than were the king and queen in their crowns and furs. France yielded to Spain and I was caught in a frenzy of flamenco dancers and gypsy guitars.

'The scene shifted to the New World where Thomas Jefferson was explaining his latest invention at Monticello, then to Baltimore where Edgar Allan Poe was mourning the death of his young bride, and then to the nation's capital where the tragic profile of Lincoln presented itself. Lincoln's features faded and those of Kennedy appeared. My eyes opened and they were filled with tears.

'As the sequence had suddenly taken a somber tone, I again closed my eyes suspecting that I was, perhaps, on the verge of a great discovery...'

'Face to face with God's image'

'It was then... that the veil was lifted for a moment and the nature of the universe was revealed. I saw nothing but a chaotic, turbulent sea. The waves were pounding, the winds were roaring, the lightning was flashing and the rains were tumbling downward in a steady torrent.

'Upon close inspection, I could see a number of tiny specks upon the sea. It was soon apparent that the specks were lifeboats and that Sarah, Al, Steve [his fellow experimenters] and myself were in one of the crafts. We clung to the side of the boat as it lurched from one wave to the next. We said not a word but our faces expressed the hopelessness of our plight. What rational purpose could possibly be expressed in our uncontrollable, aimless drifting?

'Then, in the middle of the raging, eternal sea, I came face to face with the image of God. Artists often portray God as an ancient patriarch with a beard. They are wrong. In our lifeboat we suddenly came upon God standing waistdeep in the churning waters. He was young, strong, black-haired, bare-chested; an unforgettable look of compassion, love and concern graced his facial features.

'God seemed to be telling us that He, too, was caught in the storm. To change its course was beyond His power as well as beyond ours. Nevertheless, we could be of comfort to our fellow voyagers just as He was compassionate toward us. There was little that we could do to control our course or predict our destination. Just one thing we could do and that was to love, for in the act of loving we partake of divinity.

'Once again my eyes opened. They were filled with tears; I was sobbing. My vision had been a real and vivid one, an experience of meaning and of eternal impact. I could not rest until I had phoned Dr Leary and told him of my revelation.

'The phone call completed, I realised that the mushroom experience was still upon me. I looked at the ceiling and again sobbed "because here we have the most beautiful plaster in the world..."

'...at 10:45 the numerals on my watch resumed meaning. It was then that I knew my mushroom experience was nearing its end.

'Coming "out of orbit", I faced a "re-entry problem". Re-entering my body was an uncomfortable experience. It was, in fact, the only disagreeable part of the entire evening.

'Closing my eyes, I could see the waves of letters and numbers again cascading into place, like a "verbal curtain" blotting out the extensional, non-verbal world.

'The other participants stated that this had been their deepest, most rewarding mushroom experience. After comparing impressions, our group separated and we ventured into the "outside world", the "world of reality".

'But was it a more "real" world than that which we had just experienced? I am sure it was not. I am convinced that the mushroom experience permitted us to peek beneath the veil, and to glimpse for just a moment the nature of the cosmos.'

Although Stanley Krippner does not feel that there is a substantial difference between the spontaneous and drug-induced mystic experience, this fascinating description points out the possibility of a more visual evocation of feeling in the drug-induced experience than in the spontaneous bliss experience.

Dr Stanislav Grof, towards the end of his book *Realms of the Human Unconscious* (1975), provides a possible explanation:

'In the process of consecutive LSD sessions, the major experiential focus tends to shift, by and large, from abstract and psychodynamic elements to the problems of death and rebirth, and eventually to various transpersonal sequences. Advanced LSD sessions are usually dominated by mystic and religious themes and are all transpersonal in nature; elements of the levels worked through in earlier session do not appear in this stage . . .'

As an example of this, he presents the description of an advanced LSD session with a 19-year-old schizophrenic student, 'Michael', who had relived his childhood memories in previous sessions and despite very serious clinical symptomatology, had made rapid therapeutic progress, moved through the psychodynamic stage and the perinatal stage to transpersonal levels. This was his thirty-second session.

'The session started with a feeling of "pure tension" that was building up to higher and higher levels. When the tension was transcended, Michael had an experience of overwhelming cosmic ecstasy; the universe seemed to be illuminated by radiant light emanating from an unidentifiable supernatural source. The entire world was filled with serenity, love, and peace; the atmosphere was that of "absolute victory, final liberation, and freedom in the soul."

'The scene then changed into an endless bluish-green ocean, the primordial cradle of all life. Michael felt that he had returned to the source; he was floating gently in this nourishing and soothing fluid, and his body and soul seemed to be dissolving and melting into it. The experience had a distinct Indian undertone; he asked the therapist whether this state of unity of the individual self with the universe was described in Indian religious scriptures. He saw numerous visions of Hindu worship, mourning ceremonies on the Ganges River, and Indian yogis practising in the monumental setting of the Himalayas. Without having had any previous knowledge of Hatha Yoga, Michael intuitively assumed several of the classical body postures (*asanas*) because they seemed best suited to his present state of mind.

'This ecstatic condition was suddenly interrupted and the sense of harmony deeply disturbed. The water in the ocean became amniotic fluid, and he experienced himself as a fetus in the womb. Some adverse influences·were endangering his existence [he had had a particularly traumatic childhood] ... he had a strange, unpleasant taste in his mouth, was aware of poison streaming through his body, felt profoundly tense and anxious, and various groups of muscles in his body were trembling and twitching. These symptoms were accompanied by many terrifying visions of demons and other evil appearances; they resembled those on religious painting and sculpture of various cultures. After this episode of distress passed, Michael re-experienced his own embryological development, from the fusion of the sperm and egg through millions of cell divisions and processes of differentiation to a whole individual.

'This was accompanied by an enormous release of energy and radiant light. The sequences of embryonal development were intermingled with ...flashbacks showing the transformation of animal species during the historical evolution of life.

'Toward the end of the session, Michael returned to the feelings of fusion and melting in the ocean alternating with his identification with the entire universe.' Taking many forms, some historical, his ecstasy lasted until late at night...

'The following day, he was in the calmest, most joyful and balanced emotional condition he had experienced in his entire life. After this session his psychotic symptoms never reappeared.... He has been able to take full responsibility for himself and his family and to cope successfully with all the hardships associated with the life of an emigrant.'

The *psycho*-pharmacological effects of LSD are so individual and variant, not only from person to person, but from dose to dose and from session to session, that it seems as if the chemical alterations of brain levels not only alter perception but open the door to an illimitable realm of uncharted realities.

When Dr John Lilly, an American psychoanalyst and scientist, undertook to do experimental work with LSD (as described in his book *The Center of the Cyclone*, 1972) in a tank filled with water in a soundproof, completely darkened room in which he would remain suspended for a period of several hours, he was extending his research into heightened states of awareness as experienced in isolation, solitude and confinement. His purpose was to gain insight into mystic experience as reported by saints, sages and gurus, to deepen the understanding of his own mystic experiences, which had been of immense power.

Taking a carefully prescribed amount of the drug (approximately 300 micrograins in total) he overcame his fear of surrendering all volitional grip on normal consciousness and entered the tank. The following excerpts from his account give only a glimpse of the far reaches and complexity of the experiences.

'Out beyond our galaxy'

Having established in initial experiments that he did not need a head-mask and could keep balanced and afloat, that clothing was a distraction, and there was no need to fear that he would not dissociate from his body, he fully abandoned himself to the 93°F water, the blackened silence, and the effect of the drug. He wrote:

'. . . I was still holding on to the usual cognition spaces of the body . . . the idea of a central point of identity and consciousness. Later this was found to be unnecessary, except during extreme states when I needed a rest. At these times I would return to zero point.

'This zero point is a useful place. It is not complete separation from one's previous ideas, but it is separation from the body. It is space that still represents the darkness and the silence of the tank, but with the body nonexistent . . .

'. . . suddenly I was precipitated into (universal) spaces. I maintained myself as a central point of consciousness, of feeling, of recording. I moved into universes containing beings much larger than myself so that I was a mote in their sunbeam, a small ant in their universe, a single thought in a huge mind, or a small program in a cosmic computer . . . I was swept, pushed, carried, whirled, and in general beat around by processes which I could not understand, processes of immense energy, of fantastic light, of terrifying power. My very being was threatened as I was pushed through these vast spaces by these vast entities. Waves of the equivalent of light, of sound, of motion, waves of intense emotion, were carried in dimension beyond my understanding. I became a bright luminous point of consciousness, radiating light and warmth, and know-

ledge. I moved into a space of astonishing brightness, golden light . . . I
sat in space without a body but with all of myself there . . . exhilarated
with a sense of awe, wonder, reverence. The energy surrounding me
was of incalculably high intensity . . . in the great vastness of empty
spaced filled with light . . .

. . . 'I am out beyond our galaxy, beyond galaxies as we know them.
Time is apparently speeded up by 100 billion times. The whole universe
collapses into a point. There is a tremendous explosion and out of the
point on one side comes positive matter and positive energies, streaking
into the cosmos at fantastic velocities. Out of the opposite side of the
point comes anti-matter streaking off into the opposite direction. The
universe expands to its maximum extent, recollapses, and expands three
times. . . .

'. . . I was merely an observer of microscopic size and yet I was some
part of a vast network . . . somehow responsible for what was going on.
I was given an individuality for temporary purposes only. I would be
re-absorbed into the network when the time came.'

Describing also a trip '*down*' into his own body, he writes of himself
as:

'. . . looking at various systems of organs, cellular assemblages, and
structure. I traveled among cells, watched their functioning and realized
that within myself was a grand assemblage of living organisms, all of
which added up to me. I traveled through my brain, watching the
neurons and their activities. I traveled through my heart, watching the
pulsations of the muscle cells. I traveled through my blood, watching
the business of the white blood corpuscles. I traveled down through my
gut tract, getting acquainted with the bacteria and mucosal cells in the
walls. I went into my testes and became acquainted with the formation
of the sperm cells. I then quickly moved into smaller and smaller
dimensions, down to the quantum levels and watched the play of atoms
in their own vast universes, their wide empty spaces, with the fantastic
forces involved in each of the distant nuclei with their orbital clouds of
force field electrons and the primary particles coming to this system
from outer spaces . . .'

What conclusions did Dr Lilly come to, after ten years of work in
these isolation tanks, together with many subsequent experiments and
experiences with consciousness exploration?

He cautions *against* conclusions, advocates healthy scepticism,
experiencing for oneself whatever one is attempting to discover or
convey and, above all, attempting to transcend the 'covert set of beliefs
that control one's thinking, one's actions, and one's feelings'.

'In the province of the mind, what one believes to be true either is true or becomes true within certain limits, to be found experientially and experimentally. These limits are beliefs to be transcended.'

This does not provide more than the inner evidence of what stretches invisibly from the known borders of the mind to the unknown; it leaves open-ended, at least at the present time, the question of whether or not drug-induced mystic experience is only a play of the material of transcendence, or transcendence itself.

Initially, it was hoped that LSD could simulate the symptoms of schizophrenia in normal volunteers under laboratory conditions, which might provide a key to its understanding and treatment; but in spite of certain superficial similarities there proved to be very fundamental differences between the real psychosis and its 'model' induced by drugs.

In the area of mystic experience, the schizophrenic has extremely similar feelings to both the spontaneous and the drug-induced, and as R.D. Laing, the British psychiatrist well-known for his work in this field points out in his book *The Politics of Experience* (1967), 'Madness need not be all breakdown. It may also be breakthrough. It is potentially liberation and renewal as well as enslavement and existential death.... Some psychotic people have transcendental experiences. Often (to the best of their recollection), they have never had such experiences before, and frequently they will never have them again. I am not saying, however, that psychotic experience necessarily contains this element more manifestly than sane experience...'

Dr Laing says that by categorising and segregating the inner reality from objective facts, there is a veil between "*us*" and *It* which is more like fifty feet of solid concrete....Intellectually, emotionally, inter-personally, organisationally, intuitively, theoretically, we have to blast our way through the solid wall, even if at the risk of chaos, madness and death....The person going through ego-loss or transcendental experiences may or may not become in different ways confused. But to be mad is not necessarily to be ill, notwithstanding that in our culture the two categories have become confused....The experience that a person may be absorbed in, while to others he appears simply ill-mad, may be for him veritable manna from heaven. The person's whole life may be changed, but it is difficult not to doubt the validity of such vision. Also, not everyone comes back to us again.'

'Schizophrenia not swimming but drowning'

As a commentary to this Joseph Campbell in *Myths to Live By* (1972) asks, 'What *is* the difference between a psychotic or LSD experience and a yogic, or a mystical? The plunges are all into the same deep inward sea; of that there can be of no doubt . . . but there is an important difference . . . .' It is 'equivalent simply to that between a diver who can swim and one who cannot. The mystic, endowed with native talents for this sort of thing and following, stage by stage, the instruction of a master [or the well person having a spontaneous mystic experience], enters the waters and finds he can swim; whereas the schizophrenic, unprepared (or ill-prepared), unguided, ungifted, has fallen or has intentionally plunged, and is drowning.'

And the waters in to which he has descended, Joseph Campbell says, are the archetypes of the collective unconscious, best interpreted by Carl G. Jung as 'pertaining to those structures of the psyche that are not the products of merely individual experience but are common to all mankind.' In other words, man 'has both an inherited biology and a personal biography, the "archetypes of the unconscious" being expressions of the first.'

Joseph Campbell's graphic interpretation of the 'inward schizophrenic plunge' is as follows:

'The first experience is of a sense of splitting. The person sees the world going in two: one part of it moving away; himself in the other part. This is the beginning of the regressus, the crack-off and backward flow. He may see himself, for a time, in two roles. One is the role of the clown, the ghost, the witch, the queer one, the outsider. That is the outer role that he plays, making little of himself as the fool, a joke, the one kicked around, the patsy. Inside, however, he is the saviour, and he knows it. He is the hero chosen for a destiny . . . .

'The second stage has been described in many clinical accounts. It is of a terrific drop-off and regression, backward in time and biologically as well. Falling back into his own past, the psychotic becomes an infant, a fetus in the womb . . . . the experience of slipping back to animal consciousness, into animal form, sub-animal forms, even plantlike . . . .

' . . . . In the course of a schizophrenic retreat, the psychotic too may come to know the exaltation of a union with the universe, transcending personal bounds: the "oceanic feeling" . . . . and of a new knowledge . . . . things that before had been mysterious are now fully understood. Ineffable realisations are experienced . . .' very often corresponding amazingly 'to the insights of the mystics and to the images of Hindu, Buddhist, Egyptian, and classical myth . . . .' The person who has never believed in, or heard of reincarnation may feel 'he has lived forever; that he has lived through many lifetimes, yet was never born and will never die. It is as though he had come to know himself as that Self (*atman*) of which we read in the *Bhagavad Gita*: "Never is it born, never does it die . . . Unborn, eternal, permanent, and primeval, it is not slain when the body is slain.' The patient may feel one with all things, and find surcease from sorrow, wisdom firmly fixed, at complete peace.

'In short . . . what I find that I am saying is that our schizophrenic patient is actually experiencing the same beatific ocean deep which the yogi and saint are ever striving to enjoy: except that, whereas they are swimming in it, he is drowning.'

But when a patient survives, and returns, it can be like the statement of one man who was somehow 'self-rescued' by the experience: 'When I came out, I suddenly felt that everything was so much more real than it had been before. The grass was greener, the sun was shining brighter, and people were more alive, I could see them clearer . . . .'

Joseph Campbell sums up in this way: 'The inward journeys of the mythological hero, the shaman, the mystic, and the schizophrenic are in principle the same; and when the return or remission occurs, it is experienced as a rebirth: the birth, that is to say, of a "twice-born" ego, no longer bound in by its daylight-world horizon. It is now known to be but the reflex of a larger self, its proper function being to carry the energies of an archetypal instinct system into fruitful play in a contemporary space-time daylight situation. One is no longer afraid of nature; nor of nature's child, society – which is monstrous, too, and in fact cannot be otherwise; it would otherwise not survive. The new ego is in accord with all this, in harmony, at peace; and, as those who have returned from the journey tell, life is then richer, stronger, and more joyous.'

Epilepsy and the mystic state

In the light of an exploration of mystic experience these borderlines and overlaps may be of inestimable importance. Epilepsy, like schizophrenia, is noted for its 'mystic' qualities, and research into this form of brain abnormality could well prove relevant in the quest for understanding of the nature of bliss. The comments of Dr Peter Fenwick that follow, concerning the possibility of a particular area of the brain being the source of mystic experience are of particular interest. Dr Fenwick, Consultant Neurophysiologist to St Thomas's Hospital, Bethlehem Royal Hospital, the Maudsley Hospital and the Institute of Psychiatry, in a paper contributed to this book, asks: Can any single brain structure mediate all the qualities of mystic experience? and goes on to say:

'Throughout the psychiatric literature there is without doubt an association between mystic experience and mental illness which is of interest simply because it may point towards specific structures as mediating mystic experience within the brain. Such experiences can almost certainly also rise spontaneously in the normal brain in people who have no trace of mental illness, and there is some evidence that the temporal lobes are the areas most likely to be involved. Neurosurgical operations which have been carried out in conscious patients in the treatment of epilepsy, for example, have shown that the various elements of the mystic experience can arise when different structures within the temporal lobe are stimulated.

'Further evidence for the temporal lobe origin of mystic experience comes from the very rare cases of temporal lobe epilepsy which have a positive aura. Terrifying auras are common, positive auras of either tranquility or, possibly of more importance, joy and bliss, are extremely rare. Nevertheless, their occurrence in temporal lobe epilepsy would seem to suggest yet again temporal lobe involvement in mystic experience.

'One or two cases have also been reported in which an ictal discharge (fit) arising within the non-dominant temporal lobe has given rise to a mystic experience, and certainly response is known to arise in the non-dominant temporal lobe.

'In the cases reported in the literature, it would appear that, at the time the mystic experiences arise, the discharges are confined to the non-dominant limbic system, particularly the medial temporal structures. However, it is clearly too simple just to place the source of mysticism in the right temporal lobe. A reasonable hypothesis would be that the non-dominant temporal lobe is intimately involved with the genesis of mystic experience and adds positive tone to the perception of reality which occurs during the experience itself.

'A reductionist description of mystic experience arising within the right temporal lobe gives no idea of the majesty of the experiences themselves, or the conviction that accompanies them that they are the gateway to beauty, truth and certainty.

'However, the identification of right temporal lobe structures, particularly those of the right temporal limbic structures, as being involved in the mystic experience, is at least a beginning on which reductionist science can build'.

Dr Tom Sensky, a biochemist who is senior registrar of psychiatry at The Maudsley Hospital, became interested in mystic experience when working in the epilepsy unit. In a contributing discussion of the subject,

Epilepsy, Schizophrenia and Mystic States, he writes:
'Traditionally, most physicians and psychiatrists have tended to regard mystic states as experiences exclusive to those who are unwell, either mentally or physically. Despite the growing body of evidence that many "normal" people also experience such states, this old-fashioned view remains widespread. One reason for this is the occurrence of features resembling those of mystic states in a variety of conditions of ill-health, many of which have been extensively investigated.

'To the extent that such investigations of what might be termed "unhealthy" mystic states are applicable also to similar "healthy" experiences, they may point the way to an understanding of the physiological and psychological bases of mystical states in general.

'The attribution of an epileptic basis to mystic states, being quite common, is particularly worthy of closer scrutiny. Firstly, however, it is necessary to review some salient features of epilepsy in general. Under normal circumstances, the living brain continually produces a complex of highly regulated electrical discharges which are propagated throughout its substance. Under special conditions, the regulation of these discharges can break down and an abnormal discharge may arise. This is the basis of an epileptic fit.

'Sometimes, this abnormal discharge spreads very rapidly throughout the brain giving rise to a major convulsion, the kind of fit most people associate with epilepsy; the limbs go rigid then shake, and consciousness is lost. Not all fits follow this pattern, however. Sometimes, the abnormal discharge starts in one particular part of the brain (the epileptic focus) and may then spread to adjacent areas. The way the fit manifests itself will depend on the site of the focus and the pattern of spread. For example, a focus in the part of the brain controlling movement of the fingers of one hand will initially cause these fingers to move; as the discharge spreads from the focus, the wrist will eventually begin to move, then the forearm, then the whole arm, and so on. In such a fit, consciousness may be retained. An analogous effect may be recreated during brain surgery by artificially stimulating particular areas of the brain using implanted electrodes through which a current is passed.

'With regard to mystic states, interest has centred on epileptic foci in particular areas of the brain known as the temporal lobes, of which there are two (one in either cerebral hemisphere). Epileptic attacks confined to one temporal lobe do not produce convulsions; furthermore, they may share a number of features in common with mystic states. They are often highly complex, involving altered perceptions of self, time and the world. Attacks may be associated with feelings of intense emotion. They are characteristically brief and, although they may be unheralded, can sometimes be induced.

'What happens when the temporal lobes are stimulated using implanted electrodes is also very interesting. One of their functions relates to memory and stimulation here may allow the subject to relive, as it were, apparently forgotten experiences in very vivid detail. It is not hard to imagine how superimposition of such memories, one upon another, might lead to a feeling of omniscience or unity as found in mystic states. The temporal lobes are the only areas of the brain in which such complex phenomena are produced by electrode stimulation; stimulation of other areas of the brain can only give rise to simple phenomena such as flashes of light or buzzing noises.

'The content and pattern of temporal lobe epileptic attacks will vary markedly from one individual to the next, though usually remaining constant for each. Only a small minority of temporal lobe epileptics report experiencing mystic states when they have their attacks. One could argue that it is only in these cases that the attacks have all the features necessary to allow their recognition as mystic states. Another point of view, less helpful to our purpose, is that such attacks are merely *interpreted* as mystic. Support for this alternative viewpoint comes from the fact that many epileptics who have mystic experiences associated with their seizures have a religious background before their first such experience.

'An additional problem in attempting to use temporal lobe fits as models for "healthy" mystic states is the finding that many epileptics reporting such phenomena commonly also display a schizophrenia-like state. Schizophrenia is a condition of the mind recognized by psychiatrists in which the subject experiences abnormal perceptions such as hearing voices or seeing things (these are termed hallucinations) while fully awake and conscious, and interprets his experiences in a way that leads to false conclusions, losing touch with reality.

'Although distinctions can be drawn between schizophrenic experiences and mystic ones, the differences are often quite subtle. On current evidence, it is not possible to say with any certainty that the mystic experiences reported by temporal lobe epileptics are related directly to schizophrenia, to epilepsy or to both.

'There may in fact be closer links between mystic states and schizophrenia than is commonly believed. An individual's liability to develop schizophrenia is partly under genetic control; one of the puzzles about this is why evolution should have allowed genes to survive which produce a condition of impaired reproductive capacity and dubious biological advantage. This would, however, be understandable if the same genes which predisposed to schizophrenia also, but under different circumstances, predisposed to sudden religious insights (mystic states). The value of this is based on the premise that religious beliefs play an important part in the cohesiveness of society and that these beliefs themselves are most likely to be championed by those who have had sudden religious insights. The specific link suggested is not as far-fetched as it may at first seem. One authoritative study of the families of schizophrenic women showed that their children (who had been fostered away shortly after birth and were thus away from direct maternal influence) turned out more frequently than expected to be deeply religious.

'A variety of lines of evidence point to the cardinal importance in schizophrenia of a particular region of the brain called the nucleus accumbens. This forms part of an array of nervous pathways known as the limbic system and here there is another possible link with temporal lobe epilepsy. The limbic system influences, amongst other things, emotion and motivational behaviour. There are nerve pathways connecting it with other areas of the brain dealing with various forms of sensation – visual, touch and so on. Interruption of these sensory-limbic connections results in what has been aptly termed "psychic blindness"; perceptions remain unchanged but their personal significance is altered and, in particular, their emotional connotations are lost. These sensory-limbic pathways pass through the temporal lobes, and destructive damage to both temporal lobes may result in forms of psychic blindness.

'Conversely, one attractive hypothesis aiming to explain the complexities of temporal lobe epileptic seizures suggests that the presence of an epileptic focus in the temporal lobe could induce new, extensive and excessive sensory-limbic connections. Thus a previously neutral sensory stimulus could acquire intense emotional significance. It is not hard to imagine that something similar could occur in a mystic state.

'In a brief review such as this, it is difficult not to appear dogmatic. Nearly all the observations presented here as "hard" facts need in practice to be qualified and are in any case relevant only to selected aspects of mystic experiences. Nevertheless, it is both remarkable and significant that information gathered from conditions as diverse as epilepsy and schizophrenia (to which other unusual states of mind could have been added if space permitted) could yield such a consistent picture of what might constitute an important component of the anatomical and phy-siological bases of mystic states. It may well turn out that our understanding of such states cannot be completed within the framework currently employed by science and medicine. However, this should not be allowed to deter the use of all available techniques in the quest for better under-standing.'

Yet another component of mystic experience, which is neither inconsistent nor incompatible with the foregoing, is contributed by Dr Richard Petty, a neurologist working at the Northwick Park Hospital, London:

'Understanding of the neurophysiology of mysticism may be gained from considering techniques that can be used to induce mystic states, and from examining some cases of spontaneous mystic experience.

'First, a look at a recently discovered mechanism in the deep parts of the brain stem, which is of fundamental importance in the modulation of perception.

'Spreading throughout the brain stem, from the top of the spinal cord to the deepest parts of the brain is a network of cells known collectively as the reticular system (R.S.). Within the R.S. there are two subgroups of nerve cells (neurones) each of which is a so-called neurological modulating system. These systems have the capacity to modulate any inputs to the brain – they literally "decide" what information and sensation will ultimately arrive in consciousness. Furthermore they have the capacity for modulating the very way in which groups of nerve cells, including those in the brain, function.

'At the extreme upper end of the brain stem is the so-called rostral reticular system. This has connections with all parts of the cerebral cortex. It is always active, keeping cortical neurones in a facilitated state. That is, it keeps the cortex active and receptive. The effect is global – when its activity increases, the whole cortex is stimulated.

'Now, the most powerful stimulant of the rostral reticular system is carbon dioxide, and its effect is instantaneous. During the normal cycle of respiration, there is a continuous oscillation in the amount of carbon dioxide in the blood, and consequently there is a continuous oscillation in the activity of the rostral reticular system. In patients who have persistently elevated carbon dioxide levels in the blood, for instance in severe chronic bronchitis, the whole cerebral cortex is in a state of excitation, and these people tend to be irritable and over-responsive to sensation. By way of contrast, breathing very deeply or fast lowers the carbon dioxide level, and has the effect of reducing the activity of the rostral reticular system and consequently of the whole cerebral cortex. As a result there is a reduction in ongoing perceptual experience. It is for instance well-recognised that it is easier to induce a hypnotic state if one first asks the patient to take a few deep breaths.

'The second neuronal system lies at the bottom end of the reticular system, and is responsible for selectively inhibiting inputs from any nerves in the body. It is itself modulated in several complex ways. It has been clearly demonstrated that if one locks one's attention on a single input, either sensory or mental – a thought perhaps – this has the effect of damping down all other inputs by way of these two groups of cells in the reticular system (the famous neurologist Henry Maudsley described mystic states in terms of "extreme activity of one part of the brain and extreme lassitude of the rest").

Induction techniques

'*Control of breathing*. Various breath control techniques have in several cultures and over many centuries been recommended for the induction of altered states of consciousness, and mystic experience in particular. The most elaborate system is the branch of Yoga known as Pranayama.

'There is no doubt that practitioners of the art have regularly achieved mystic states, as well as performing extraordinary physical feats. Each type of breathing exercise revolves around the stimulation and circulation of "Prana" – an energy found particularly in air. One of the best known exercises is called the "Yoga cleansing Breath", and involves a series of deep, controlled, rhythmic breaths.

'In each case, the carbon dioxide concentration in the blood is markedly lowered, and, as we have seen, this has the effect of reducing the activity of the rostral reticular system, and so reducing the ongoing perceptual experience in the cerebral cortex. This will, of itself, induce an inward-turning of attention, which, as will be seen, provides one of the main neurological pre-conditions necessary for the induction of mystic experience.

'*Chanting*. This technique has been recommended by a number of schools, most well known being the esoteric order of Zoroastrianism, and some Sufi schools. It is probably also one factor in the experience of some Christian mystics who reported the development of the state after chanting of prayers, psalms and hymns.

'The important feature here is of repetitive stimulation of the reticular system, and hence in the cerebral cortex, due to a phenomenon known as "Habituation". It has been clearly demonstrated that any form of repetitive stimulation will cause a reduction in the activity of neurones – in effect they become "bored", and consequently the cerebral cortex is generally inhibited. This again produces the necessary pre-conditions for the mystic experience. It is highly likely that this same phenomenon of habituation occurs with some other induction techniques, in particular the clicking of the prayer wheels of Tibetan Buddhists, and the use of the Catholic rosary.

'*Dance and Movement*. Morihei Uyeshiba, the inventor of Aikido told of a mystic experience which occurred spontaneously, soon after performing a series of Katas – ritualised martial arts exercises. In this case he was one of the greatest exponents of the art, and it is clear that he had achieved such a degree of proficiency in the exercises that he was able to perform them without conscious thought. In several of the martial arts this is called the state of "No mind". This again suggests that the experience occurred during a time when his cerebral cortex was maximally inhibited.

'A similar phenomenon is said to occur during the performances of accomplished Dervish dancers. More highly complex series of movements are performed in a state of total absorption and without conscious thought, again suggesting inhibition of the cortex. The same principle applies in the system of Hatha Yoga, where specific Asanas (postures) and Mudras (gestures) are used to induce altered states of consciousness.

'*Light*. One of the best known cases of spontaneous mystic experience is that of Jacob Boehme, who, in 1600, at the age of twenty-five, entered the state after staring briefly at an intense light – the sun reflected on a burnished pewter dish. It is possible to create a neurological map to explain at least some of what happened.

'Light enters the eye and is coded into electrical signals which are carried to the visual cortex at the back of the brain. From here signals enter the reticular system as well as several other parts of the brain. This massive input from only one type of sensory stimulus would cause damping of the reticular system and hence of the cortex, again creating the necessary pre-conditions for the mystic experience.

'Some schools of meditation have recommended intense concentration on a single object, the most popular being a candle, with the intention of achieving a mystic state of consciousness. This again has the effect of damping the reticular system by providing only one type of sensory input. It is of considerable interest that during this exercise one often notices changes in the intensity of light, which is strong evidence for the phenomenon of habituation occurring, most probably in the reticular system.

'*Biofeedback*. There is some evidence that sophisticated forms of biofeedback [defined on page 105 below] may be used to induce altered states of consciousness, including the mystic experience. With this technique, people are made aware of certain physical processes within themselves, by the use of some form of monitor – usually a modified type of electro-encephalograph (EEG) which measures the brain's electrical activity. They are then taught to change the readings on the monitor, and therefore of the internal process by use of willpower and concentration.

'It is not known precisely how this process works, but most of the recorded phenomena indicate that there is a kind of improved co-ordination between various parts of the brain. This is unlikely to be due to increased arousal within the cerebral cortex, since, as has been shown here, this would tend to lead to irritability and excitability, but is more like to be the consequence of global cortical damping.

'This would allow the emergence of stable patterns within the cortex, since normal sensory inputs are being reduced to a minimum, and it is normally these sensory inputs which induce cortical instability.

'Cortical damping of this type may, as we have seen, be induced by the rostral reticular system. It is of great interest that it has recently been shown that there are at least two groups of cells in the frontal lobes which project to the reticular system, and are able to modulate its activity. There is a good deal of evidence that the frontal lobes are intimately associated with the execution of will-power and concentration, and so we have here a rather elegant explanation for the way in which biofeedback may be used to induce an altered state of consciousness.

'*Mantra.* The use of Mantra – constant inner repetition of a sound, word or phrase – is very widely used for inducing altered states of con-sciousness. Superficially the technique would appear closely related to chanting, but the fundamental difference is that the mantra is not verbalised. The whole process occurs within the mind. The mechanism by which this has its effect is almost certainly the same as that seen with the other techniques – namely repetitive stimulation of the rostral reticular system causing habituation and thus cortical damping. On this occasion the repetitive stimulation of the reticular system is again mediated by the pathways from the frontal lobes of the brain to the reticular system, which are involved in the biofeedback mechanism.'

The first coherent explanation

'It has been stated that reduction in cerebral cortical activity creates a pre-condition for the mystic experience. There is still the question of what actually happens after this has occurred.

'In recent years it has become fashionable to ascribe the mystic experience to the right or non-dominant cerebral hemisphere. This is an interesting concept which is based on the postulated functions of this hemisphere, which are alleged to be holistic, intuitive and creative. The evidence for this is very incomplete, and in some cases certainly represents an unjustified extrapolation from known facts.

'The appeal of this "Two hemisphere" approach is in many ways related to a natural desire to find a location in the brain for two aspects of psychology which have tended to be ignored in recent years – the intellectual and intuitive. However, a consideration of the actual, known functions of each hemisphere makes it clear that there is very considerable overlap in function and activity between the two sides of the brain.

'A simple example is this: In most of the older neurological textbooks it is said that the recognition of faces, which involves a holistic perception, is clearly localised within the right hemisphere. It is now known that both hemispheres have this capacity, apparently to the same degree.

'The effect of the reticular system is global – it affects both hemispheres equally, and although this may cause a suppression in the normally dominant left hemisphere, allowing the right hemisphere to assert itself, there is absolutely no evidence for this. Another mechanism is required to explain the appearance of altered states of consciousness, and of mystic experience in particular. A very attractive solution is provided by the eminent but controversial neuropsychologist Karl Pribram (see pages 110-12 below).

'He has developed a theory, for which there is now considerable evidence, that at least some parts of the brain – specifically those involved in memory and perception work in a way analogous to that seen with a holographic camera. Basically, it is known that when the junctions between nerve cells – synapses – are activated in the brain, that this never occurs in isolation, but huge numbers of synapses are activated simultaneously, and this creates a "Wavefront" in the brain.

'These wavefronts are made up of changes in electrical potential at the fine branches of nerve endings. Because these waves are coming from different directions, they interact and produce interference patterns, in exactly the same way as ripples on a pond interact and interfere. Basically neurones work in two ways – they may be on or off, or they may develop "Graded slow potentials" – a gradual build up of current at nerve endings, and it is this second mechanism which creates the wavefronts. The result is that information is distributed throughout the brain and not just in small, localised areas, and more importantly for our purposes, it means that at one stage of processing performs its analyses in the frequency domain – the realm of wave interference.

'In this domain neither time nor space exist per se. This of course sounds very much like one of the fundamental features of the mystic experience. It would therefore seem that the mind can enter this domain, but only when the normal activity of the cerebral cortex is damped down, allowing uninterrupted, co-ordinate holographic functioning.

'This is a very elegant theory, and is almost certainly true on at least one level, and is probably the first coherent explanation for mystic experience in scientific terms.'

The Measure of Bliss

'... We will have to improve our general awareness quite a lot before we can really appreciate what a benefit the East-West, ancient-modern synthesis of self-awareness and self-control will be for humanity' – C. Maxwell Cade and Nona Coxhead, *The Awakened Mind* (1979)

One factor that all forms of meditation and contemplation seem to have in common is *attention*, the concentrated focus of the mind. Could it be this invisible monitoring that initiates or activates the 'wavefronts', that are ultimately the 'damping down' which allows the 'uninterrupted, co-ordinate functioning' of Karl Pribram's fascinating hypothesis? Arthur J. Deikman, psychiatrist and psychoanalyst, wrote an article in 1964, entitled *Deautomatization and the Mystic Experience*, which has a continuing relevance to contemporary consideration of this crucial factor.

'Automatization' in human beings can be broadly defined as the process by which a learned function, e.g. driving a car, or a learned 'goal orientation', such as earning a great deal of money or experiencing physical pleasure, drops below the level of consciousness and becomes automatic. Thus a human being who has become 'automatized' as far as the function of car driving is concerned will accelerate or change gear when road conditions call for these actions without consciously doing so. Similarly, someone with an 'automatized goal orientation' towards, say, physical pleasure moves toward his or her goal like an automaton, regardless and even unconscious of future consequences. At its worst, as in the case of a psychopath, such an automatization is pathological.

'Deautomatization' is simply the undoing of the automatic structure and can be the preliminary to either progress or regress. Thus a car driver's deautomatization, a resumption of *conscious* and deliberate gear changing, acceleration etc., can be either regressive, as in the case of someone driving with great attention because he or she is suffering from the effects of alcohol or disease, or progressive, as in the case of someone learning to handle a new and more powerful vehicle.

In reference to mystical contemplation Dr Deikman wrote:

'In reflecting on the technique of contemplative meditation, one can see that it seems to constitute just such a manipulation of attention as is required to produce deautomatization. The percept receives intense attention while the use of attention for abstract categorization and thought is explicitly prohibited. Since automatization normally accomplishes the transfer of attention *from* a percept of action to abstract thought activity, the meditation procedure exerts a force in the reverse direction. Cognition is inhibited in favor of perception; the active intellectual style is replaced by a receptive perceptual mode.'

The effect of this, he says, is that, according to H. Werner, ' " . . . The image . . . gradually changes in functional character. It becomes essentially subject to the exigencies of abstract thought. Once the image changes in function and becomes an instrument in reflective thought, its structure will also change. It is only through such structural change that the image can serve as an instrument of expression in abstract mental activity. This is why, of necessity, the sensuousness, fullness of detail, the color and vivacity of the image must fade." . . . and it is striking to note that classical accounts of mystic experience emphasize the phenomenon of Unity. Unity can be viewed as a dedifferentiation that merges all boundaries until the self is no longer experienced as a separate object and customary perceptual and cognitive distinctions are no longer applicable. In this respect, the mystic literature is consistent with the deautomatization process.

'A final comment should be made. The content of the mystic experience reflects not only its unusual mode of consciousness but also the particular stimuli being processed through that mode. . . . Such an explanation says nothing conclusive about the source of "transcendent" stimuli. God or the Unconscious share equal responsibilities here and one's interpretation will reflect one's presuppositions and beliefs . . .

' . . . Yet for psychological science, the problem of understanding such internal processes is hardly less complex than the theological problem of understanding God. Indeed, regardless of one's direction in the search to know what reality is, a feeling of awe, beauty, reverence, and humility seem to be the product of one's efforts. Since these emotions are characteristic of the mystic experience itself, the question of the epistemological [metaphysical] validity of that experience may have less importance than was initially supposed.'

In a more recent work, *The Observing Self*, Arthur J. Deikman further suggests that Western psychology has failed to acknowledge the mystical, observing, or 'core self' of those they attempt to help, and that the greatest gift it could make to psychotherapy would be to incorporate the teaching parables of the mystic traditions – to permit new development of the intuitive perception 'which provides access to meaning.' He also advocates meditation, which he believes could help to develop the 'observing self'.

Ralph Waldo Emerson, the 19th-century New England philosopher once said: 'A man should learn to detect and watch that gleam of light which flashes across his mind from within, more than the lustre of the firmament of bards and sages.'

Monitoring the body during Bliss

In her special research, Hazel Guest, a British psychotherapist with her own practice, was able to monitor such 'flashes' as they occurred during sessions of sequential analysis (a form of analysis designed by Dr I.N. Marshall) to capture and measure them in physiological-psychological correlation. She describes her work as follows:

'It is only recently that altered states of consciousness have become a subject for scientific study, the earliest of these studies concentrating on the physiological changes that take place during dreaming and deep sleep. There is no problem about deciding whether a person is asleep or not; but in order to know whether he is dreaming, it is necessary to waken him and ask. A subjective element has now crept into the experiment, and this is something which the traditional scientific method does not permit. Researchers in this field have had to adopt a new approach, and accept that the only person who can say whether or not he has experienced an altered state of consciousness, is the subject himself. Charles Tart, humanistic and experimental psychologist of the University of California, noted for his work in this field has written: "An altered state of consciousness (ASC) may be defined as a qualitative alteration in the overall pattern of mental functioning, such that the experiencer feels his consciousness is radically different from the 'normal' way it functions."

'Altered states include dreaming, deep sleep, the half-awake hypnagogic (just falling asleep) and hypnopompic (just waking up) states, deep meditation, the sudden "peak experience", trance, hypnosis, psychedelic states, alcoholic intoxication, and psychotic states. Of these, the two which are of concern here are the transcendental states of deep meditation and the peak experience.

'The first is a state of deep but wakeful relaxation that is usually entered as the result of engaging in some appropriate meditational practice; the second is sudden and unplanned, and is the result of a flash of insight or of a new and significant experience. Although these two states of consciousness [i.e., mystic and peak experience states] are entered into quite differently, once one is there they are experienced as being similar, and are often incorrectly described as being the same state.

'There are marked physiological differences between them which will be described later; but for the moment I will treat them together, describing those aspects in which they are alike.

'The earliest and most significant research, so far, into the subjective qualities of these experiences was done by Dr Abraham Maslow (1968). First and foremost they are ego-less states, that is to say there is no longer any distinction between self and the environment – hence the terms "transcendental" and the "oceanic experience"....An observer would probably see certain physical changes, especially on the face, such as an expression of happiness and calm, with a youthful radiance.

'As soon as any scientific attempt is made to monitor physiological functions during transcendental states of consciousness the differences between the two states mentioned above become important. First of all there is the question of inducing the state so that it can be observed. It is easy enough to select a number of practising meditators and ask them to get on with it; but you cannot arrange for someone to have a spontaneous peak (or mystic) experience to order.

'Consequently most of the physiological research has been done on meditators. It has been found that their electrical brain rhythms become slower, their consumption of oxygen is reduced, and their electrical skin resistance climbs steadily up. Peak experiences, on the other hand, are spontaneous; but in spite of this there are certain techniques which tend to produce insights of the "peak" kind, e.g., the Zen *Koan* [a question the Master asks the student monk, which must be answered, but which has no logical answer, such as what is the sound of one hand clapping?].

'The writer uses techniques designed for use in counselling sessions, which tend to produce these flashes of insight. In these sessions the phenomenon is described as a "release", because its effect is the subsequent re-orientation of the patient's thinking in relation to the insight. Since skin-resistance meters are often used as monitoring devices during these sessions, the skin-resistance phenomena associated with the release state have been observed many times. The resistance comes down very suddenly at the moment of the flash of insight. It then stays down low during the altered state, with a complete absence of any of the instantaneous perturbations that are usually present during the normal state of consciousness; in fact, the needle of the meter has the appearance of floating freely.

'This is in marked contrast to the phenomenon observed during meditation, in which the skin-resistance creeps slowly up and up. In

Zen (meditation) the ASC [altered state of consciousness] immediately following such a flash of insight or enlightenment, is called *Satori*, and is carefully distinguished from the meditation state, *Samadhi*. It should be remembered, however, that it is possible to go suddenly into the state of *Satori* from that of *Samadhi*.

'Because releases occur spontaneously and unexpectedly, most are not monitored by any physiological device at the time of their occurrence. However, it is possible to *recall* a release state subsequently, simply by remembering the insight and by getting back into the *feeling* of it. The skin resistance will not suddenly drop, because there is no new insight, but it will show the freely floating motion if the subject is re-experiencing the release state. This is one way of verifying that a former experience was indeed that of release.'

Having had several profound mystic experiences herself, Hazel Guest concludes: 'Most people who have had a transcendental experience agree that it is very difficult to describe, which is because there is nothing else with which it can be compared. But for this reason, also, a great deal of nonsense is talked about these states by people who have not experienced them.

'One common mistake is to confuse them with the psychedelic experience induced by taking LSD or some similar drug. Another, is to write off all who claim to have had a transcendental experience as psychotic. Of course, some experiences during an LSD trip are transcendental, and some people who have transcendental experiences are also psychotic [see Joseph Campbell's comments on page 90]. It is possible to go from one altered state to another; the route to an ASC is not necessarily straight from the normal waking state.

'It is also true that there are people who, for various reasons of their own, claim to have had transcendental ASC's when they have not. However, all this should not be allowed to invalidate the true transcendental experience, which is a blissful state while it lasts, and leaves the subject feeling greatly enriched.'

Biofeedback and 'State Five'

C. Maxwell Cade, scientist, and pioneer British researcher in the use of biofeedback augmented by Eastern meditative techniques, agrees that one state may lead to another and that even *satori* has gradations – 'it may take a great many satoris,' he says, 'to make one Enlightenment. We have made some progress in the measurement of brain-waves in *Samahdi*, but it is, of course, slow because the state itself is sudden, unexpected, brief. We have, however, found that occurrence of State

Five always precedes sudden excursions into other realms.'

To explain what he means by 'State Five', it is necessary to review the principle of biofeedback itself, then relate it to the particular way in which he applies it in his work.

Biofeedback is the science of 'listening to the body' with the aid of electronic instruments which monitor its changes, such as the electrical activity of the brain, and 'feed back' the information by means of a registering needle, an audible tone – or, as in the case of the most sophisticated of the instruments, the 'Mind Mirror' – various patterns formed on the panels of the instrument by light-emitting diodes.

In his book *The Awakened Mind* (with Nona Coxhead), Maxwell Cade describes how this measuring and recording, as well as what is personally felt leads to conviction of a mind-body unity and is the 'doorway to a new, expanded realm of self-control and self-unfolding'.

'. . . If one is enabled physically to observe in one's self some biological happening of which one is not normally aware, for example the presence of what is called the alpha rhythm in one's brain waves, then one can be trained to control that happening. In cases of alpha rhythm, the subject may be trained to produce at will more of the appropriate state of calm, detached awareness with which it is associated. So as one aspect of biofeedback is the training of the individual to control his state of awareness, just as one aspect of the Eastern philosophies of yoga, Sufism or Zen is the training of the individual to control his own internal awareness at will, it might reasonably be said that biofeedback is an instrumented mystic self-control.

While incorporating all the basic principles and techniques of biofeedback as a medical tool for the control of psychosomatic and stress-related diseases, Maxwell Cade branched off into this singular emphasis, combining training and monitoring with the ancient art of meditation, so as to achieve maximal mind-body awareness.

In putting some 4000 students through his classes, instructing them in the art of meditation, providing 'guided imagery', monitoring the machines they were wired to, he gradually discerned a 'hierarchy' of states of awareness, each with physiological correlates. The top one was State Five, just above the Fourth State of traditional meditation and of the 'relaxation response'.

A more precise instrument was needed to learn more about these states, particularly as to those above Five. With the help of the brilliant electronic engineer who worked with him, Geoffrey Blundell of Audio Ltd., the 'Mind Mirror' was devised. This machine can monitor not only muscle tone and the standard cycles of brain waves, but can differentiate between the activity of the right and left hemispheres of the brain.

The training was now directed toward particular methods of meditation, to left and right brain hemisphere exercises designed to achieve discrimination between them and attain more evidence of brain-hemisphere EEG 'symmetry'. Describing their feelings as they reached State Five, or at times, State Six, students sounded more and more like mystics. People who had no mystic inclination or artistic abilities created beautiful drawings, or wrote ecstatic poetry, or wept with joy. 'Some six "Enlightenments" have occurred by themselves', Maxwell Cade observes, and concludes in his contributive words for this book, 'I feel we must be in at least a meditative state – possibly State Five or State Six – to feel the true characteristics of such a Feeling. The use of both hemispheres of the brain is clearly indicated and also, to get Jung's sense of the "wholeness" of things, of both parts of the limbic system and of the brain stem as well. That seems to be the only way in which we can get a clear sense of its "coming from" anywhere!'

Dr Peter Fenwick concurs in some measure, from the viewpoint of neurophysiology: '. . .the brain should be viewed as a whole and the evidence suggests that during the mystic experience new patterns of neural activity affecting both hemispheres occur and that the experience arises because of a change in balance between hemisphere functioning. Possibly training methods alter the overall activation of the brain so that the new patterns may emerge. Certainly there is evidence to suggest that the mystic experience can be induced by procedures which tend to bring the hemispheres into balance.'

The duration of Bliss

It is perhaps a change of the person himself, rather than the alteration of the alpha levels or change in balance of the brain hemispheres that precedes all measurement. Peter Russell, scientist, author, and teacher of Transcendental Meditation, contributes the following experience and theories:

As with Maxwell Cade's 'gradations' of enlightenment' he says not all such experiences are sudden, and as in his own case given here, were built up slowly. 'Maharishi was conducting a meditation teacher's course in Majorca and having a long Christmas break I spent three weeks with the course. Before returning home, I went to say a quick goodbye to Maharishi, and also to get his views about something I had been pondering over.

'. . .I left feeling the by then familiar kind of high which comes from a personal contact and blessing from "the master".

'Two hours later I was sitting in a plane on the runway at Palma airport and the high seemed to be getting stronger . . . it was like some still but strong energy flowing through my chest. Needless to add that mentally I was feeling in a very good state; full of joy, not towards anything in particular, but more towards everything – the joy of being alive.'

Peter Russell's experience, which was to some extent shared by those with whom he was associated, continued for about a week after his return home. He comments:

'This state, with its contagion, lasted for about a week in all. The first three days were the strongest, and then it slowly decreased in intensity over the rest of the week. Yet it remains a most vivid memory.

'What also remains is the knowledge that such states are possible, not only individually, but also *collectively*. That one person's higher consciousness can directly elicit another's. It's what the Indians call "darshan", and maybe one of the great challenges of our time is finding ways to allow it to happen more easily and more widely.

'How can *such* experiences relate to activity in the brain? First, we have to understand the types of neural activity which lie behind conscious experience in general. That there is an intimate relationship between the physical activity of the brain and conscious experience is a fundamental postulate of modern psychology, but the exact nature of this relationship still largely eludes us.

'We know that some very general patterns of neural activity can be correlated with certain states of consciousness (wakeful, alertness, deep sleep, epileptic seizure, coma, etc., each producing characteristic traces in the EEG) and we know that stimulation of specific areas of the brain will generally produce the same class of experience. But we know very little about why or how a particular brain state gives rise to one particular conscious experience.

'It is extremely unlikely that the activity of a few neurons alone is responsible for a conscious experience: it is almost certain that a highly complex activity involving millions of cells is necessary. Such an activity would take a small but finite time to be generated. Various lines of approach suggest that this time is of the approximate order of one tenth of a second.

'One tenth of a second may seem a very brief time, but by neurological standards it is fairly long. When we consider that one neuron is able to excite another in about one millisecond and that each neuron may interact with a thousand or more others it rapidly becomes apparent that an immensely complex activity can be established in one hundred milliseconds. A simplified mathematical analysis shows that the potential number of interactions that could be made by the brain in a tenth of a second far exceeds the number of atoms in the Universe.

'And so, in this one infinitesimally brief moment of time, a most complex pattern of activity is generated throughout the cortex, and our conscious experience seems to depend on the coherence and patterning of this activity.

'One hypothesis is that the more ordered the activity across the cortex becomes, the stronger the associated conscious experience. In cybernetic terms the progressive complexification of neural activity represents an increase in signal-to-noise ratio. In this case the signal is the coherent activity, the noise is the more random background activity. When a certain degree of coherence is attained through the cortex, the signal becomes differentiable from the other on-going activity in the brain and emerges as a conscious experience. There is in effect a threshold for conscious experience. Less coherent activity will be masked out by the other activity and will remain below the threshold.

'How does this relate to mystic experience? A common characteristic of such experiences is that they happen when the person is in a relaxed quiet receptive state of mind. Indeed, nearly all meditation techniques whose goal is to facilitate such states of consciousness are designed, in one way or another to help the mind and body settle down into a state of profound quiet. We should expect, therefore, that the general level of neural "noise" in the brain is reduced in such states of consciousness, with the result that patterns of activity which were not previously coherent enough to stand out against the background noise, now reach consciousness.

'The subjective correlate would be that the person begins to notice subtler qualities of his or her experience. When the nervous system is very active or over-stimulated we tend to feel jangly, and perceive only the more superficial aspect of the world around us. If extremely excited we may even experience some form of tunnel vision and only be aware of those aspects we are concentrating on. Everything else has been overshadowed. Conversely when the mind is quiet, we feel at peace, and in this peace may be much more aware of the beauty of the world around us.

What is holography?
Peter Russell considers that the above hypothesis is supported by the holographic theory of brain functioning. Before reading what he has to

say about this, it might be useful to describe in simple terms the actual process of holography. What it illustrates and what it implies is elaborated in more detail later, but these excerpts from *The Holographic Paradigm – and other paradoxes*, edited by Ken Wilber (1982), give an initial idea:

'A hologram (that which results from the lensless photography) is a special type of optical storage system that can best be explained by an example: if you take a holographic photo of, say, a horse, and cut out one section of it, e.g., the horse's head, and then enlarge that section to the original size, you will get, not a big head, but a picture of the *whole* horse. In other words, each individual part of the picture contains the whole picture in condensed form. The part is in the whole and the whole is in each part – a type of unity-in-diversity and diversity-in-unity. The key point is simply that the *part* has access to the *whole* . . . . and, if the hologram is broken, any piece will reconstruct the entire image.'

There is some evidence that memories are stored in the brain in a similar way to that in which visual images are stored on a holographic plate. When a person suffers a substantial loss of brain tissue, for instance, there is not usually a total loss of a segment of memory, as would be expected if individual memories were stored in individual cells or groups of cells. Instead, all or most memories persist: even if blurred as in an incomplete holographic print, a small piece of a holographic print still holds the entire image of its subject.

Writing of the holographic theory of memory in connection with his hypothesis about the bliss experience, Peter Russell continues:

'. . . When an image is reproduced from a hologram the clarity of the image is dependent upon the coherence of the light which formed the corresponding interference pattern. If there is a large degree of background visual "noise" in the hologram this affects the detail and preciseness of the final image.

'If the holographic model of mind is valid then it would appear that during these higher states of consciousness the hologram is becoming person is moving completely beyond sensory experience (i.e. experience of any particular image in the hologram) and beginning to function at the level of pure consciousness, consciousness without object of experience.

'This goes some way towards explaining the universality and connectedness felt in such states. All the images in a hologram linked together at the level of the pure coherent light which is the substratum of each particular image.

'Pure consciousness would be the correlate of this image in the human mind, and would correspond to a high degree of coherence in the neural activity. And the EEG evidence from long term practitioners of meditation suggest that this is indeed the case.'

While the monitoring, measuring, recording of the moments of transcendent bliss in pursuit of its physiological correlates is entering ever more subtle realms, such as the 'energy fields' associated with the *chakras* in the Kundalini effect (see page 65), Chinese acupuncture meridians, and many other areas of mind-brain-body coherence, electronic exploration progresses only by means of increased sensitivity of machinery, effective modes of experimentation, aggregation of statistical evidence.

But theorizing does not have to wait on proof, and in relation to brain functioning and mystic experience there is widespread interest in the holographic hypothesis referred to by Peter Russell and Dr Richard Petty in connection with the ideas of Karl H. Pribram, Professor of Neuroscience at Stanford University, California, and author of the classic in this field, *Languages of the Brain*.

In the journal *ReVision* (1978), Karl Pribram told how holography tied-in to his research findings in work with location of memory in the brain. 'Specific memories,' he wrote, 'are incredibly resistant to brain damage. Removing a hunk of brain tissue or injuring one or another portion of the brain does not excise a particular memory or set of memories. The process of remembering may be disturbed in some general way, or even some aspect of the general process may be disrupted. But never is a single memory trace of some particular experience lost while all else that is memorable is retained.

'This fact has become well established both through clinical observation in man and through experiment on animals. Thus in some way or other memory must become distributed – the experienced input from the senses becomes spread over a sufficient expanse of brain to make the memory of that experience resistant to brain damage....'

Karl Pribram was the first to whom it seemed plausible that the distributed memory store of the brain might resemble a holographic record. He wrote: 'I developed a precisely formulated theory based on known neuroanatomy and known neurophysiology that could account for the brain's distributed memory store in holographic terms.'

In the intervening years since then, he says, 'Many laboratories including my own have provided evidence in support of parts of this theory. Other data have sharpened the theory and made it an even more precise fitting to the known facts.'

Karl Pribram went on to interpret the entire universe in terms of holography. He argued that the brain is itself a hologram containing a complete image of a holographic universe in which everything is at once everywhere and, in a sense, contains everything else. In such a universe it would be impossible to separate or 'select out' any one part of total reality, for the part would always contain the whole as the whole contains the part.

'. . . .Perhaps the most profound insight gained from holography is the reciprocal relationship between the frequency (holographic) domain and the image/object domain – recall that the fundamental question under consideration is whether mind results as an emergent property from the interaction of an organism with its environment – or whether mind reflects the basic organization of the universe (including the organism's brain . . .)

'What is organism (with its component organs) is no longer sharply distinguished from what lies outside the boundaries of the skin. In the holographic domain, each organism represents in some manner the universe, and each portion of the universe represents in some manner the organism within it . . . . The perceptions of an organism cannot be understood without an understanding of the nature of the physical universe and the nature of the physical universe cannot be understood without an understanding of the observing perceptual process.

'It is thus the fact that the holographic domain is reciprocally related to the image/object domain that implies that mental operations (such as mathematics) reflect the basic order of the universe.'

He adds that one characteristic of the holographic order is of special interest: 'This domain deals with the density of occurrences only; time and space are collapsed in the frequency domain . . . .the ordinary boundaries of space and time, location in space and in time become suspended and must be "read out" when transformations into the object/ image domain are effected. In the absence of space-time coordinates, the usual causality upon which most scientific explanation depends must also be suspended. Complementarities, synchronicities (seeming coincidences), symmetries, and dualities must be called upon as explanatory principles.

'. . .whether mind, consciousness and psychological properties in general are emergents or expressions of some basic ordering principle rests on which of two reciprocally related domains is considered primary, the image/object or the implicate holographic.

'Perhaps if the rules for "tuning in" on the holographic, implicate domain could be made more explicit, we could come to some agreement as to what constitutes the primary basic order of the universe. At the moment this order appears so indistinguishable from the mental operations

by which we operate on that universe that we must conclude either that
our science is a huge mirage, a construct of the emergent of our convoluted
brains, or that, indeed, as proclaimed by all great religious convictions,
a unity characterizes this emergent and the basic order of the universe.'
Are there whispers here of mysticism? Echoes of William Blake? :

'To see a world in a Grain of Sand
And a Heaven in a Wild Flower
Hold Infinity in the palm of your hand
And Eternity in an hour.'

Of St. Augustine?:

'God is a circle whose centre is everywhere and His circumference is
nowhere.'

Mystical experience, Karl Pribram has observed, is no more strange
than many other phenomena in nature, such as the selective repression
of DNA to form first one organ, then another. "If we get ESP or paranor-
mal phenomena in physics – it simply means that we are reading out
of some other dimension at that time. In our ordinary way we can't
understand that.' But, in time, he predicts, 'the soft sciences of today will
be the core of hard science, just as cognitive psychology, once considered
soft, took precedence over behaviorism.... Productive scientists must
be as ready to defend spirit as data... The days of the cold-hearted,
hard-headed technocrat appear to be numbered.'

The implicate enfolded order

New notions of space, time and matter have for many years been
developed by Professor David Bohm, eminent theoretical physicist of
Birkbeck College, London, who worked with Einstein. His theory of the
universe is presented fully in his book, *Wholeness and the Implicate
Order* (1980).

In his boldly conceived 'Implicate Enfolded Order', in which the
movement consists of unfolding an order which is folded up, and therefore
not a movement in space or time at all, Professor Bohm proposes that
the ways mind works are similar to the ways matter works, that the
universe works in a way that is not all that different from the way
consciousness works, that all matter has a kind of consciousness, that
'consciousness is a reflection of reality'.

To understand his theory it is helpful to draw an analogy from
nature. Let us think of a mature oak tree, perhaps a century or more old.
Looking at it from the ordinary point of view it is clearly the product of
movement in time and space. It has grown outwards and upwards –
motion in space – and it has suffered the wear and tear of events, has

matured, and thus moved in time.

In a sense, however, spatial and temporal motions are illusory. For the mature tree can be seen as having been present in 'enfolded form' in the acorn from which it grew. Under the stimuli of sun, light, and air the acorn was 'unfolded' to present (to 'display' in Professor Bohm's term) first a shoot, then a sapling, then a young tree and finally the mature oak. In other words, whatever may be 'displayed', i.e. is capable of being observed at a particular moment, by the oak it is merely an unfolding of the 'enfolded order' of the original acorn. This process works 'backwards' as well as 'forwards' – the mature tree enfolds the original acorn quite as surely as the latter 'enfolds' the former.

'. . .Quantum mechanics', he says, 'implies that there are discontinuous transitions from one state to another, without passing through the states in between. Now that would imply that the nature of time, space and matter cannot be separated . . .the past does not become the present, something new is eternally unfolding – this unfolding is the way in which the past, present and future may be folded all together, that which is implicate, in all its content, becomes "explicate", or unfolded.'

Professor Bohm, in tandem with Karl Pribram's theory, illustrates this idea with the hologram, in which, he explains, 'we can form an image in which everything is 'implicit', that is to say folded into each part, and can become unfolded by using light in a suitable way so that you can see a three-dimensional image coming out. The image is 'frozen' in each part of the picture. It is characteristic of this 'holomovement' (or 'indivisible flux') that the whole is in each part, that there is no division of the world.

In developing this new general world view, Professor Bohm says: 'We cannot stop with the attempt to understand matter alone through the implicate order. For we ourselves, along with electrons, protons, rocks, planets, galaxies, etc. are only relatively stable forms in the holomovement. It is necessary to include not only our bodies, with their brains and nervous systems, but also our thoughts, feelings, urges, will and desire, which are inseparable from the functions of these brains and nervous systems. If the ultimate ground of all matter is in the implicate order, as contained in the holomovement, it thus seems inevitable that what has generally been called "mind" must also have the same ultimate ground.'

Taking his explorative theory even further into the 'immeasurable' concept of the holomovement, Professor Bohm, in a taped interview for this book, allowed himself to speculate on its relation to mystic experience, in particular the experience of bliss:

'People may have a true or false experience of bliss. It has been found that hormones can induce it, or drugs such as morphine...but if it could be explained by chemistry it would not be worth very much, and if explained only as emotion, it could be false.

'You have to ask the question, is this a true perception? The word mystic means basically something hidden. Mystery. What is hidden and who is hiding it? Well, it is not really hidden, it is simply that from the so-called normal point of view, the one from which we could understand it, would mean to suppose that the normal state of consciousness hides something deeper from itself. Perhaps when it ceases to hide we will see something beyond. They [bliss experiences] may be to a certain extent a reaction to the anxious in the normal state. Merely removing anxiety or pain will cause pleasure, e.g., stubbing your toe, as the pain goes away there is a reaction of pleasure.

'If you could say very much about this state then it would not mean very much – if you could explain it. But what you might hope to explain is why the *normal state* is there, getting in the way. I could make one more point – from the view of the enfolded order – reality is enfolded in unknown depths of inwardness. It unfolds in consciousness and displays itself. It unfolds to reveal something rather than for the sake of itself. Like the plant unfolds, produces the seed, produces the tree but it's not exactly revealing the seed. When you display something you lay it out on the table to show what it is.

'Consciousness is primarily a show or display of something deeper. The mistake that is made is [to perceive] what is *displayed* as that which *is*.

'The explicate or unfolded order is taken to be the order of reality. In that case, everything is external to other human beings, to nature and to whatever else exists. So this would create a sense of isolation. This would produce unhappiness and anxiety. We might say the truth is, perhaps, that this is only a display and that there is something whole and deeper which is all folded together, as one.

'If that is the case, the perception of that would free the mind from fear, anxiety and unhappiness which comes from the notion of separation and danger and all that goes with it. If that is a correct perception, the mind will correctly perceive for some reason the deeper order rather than see it in its present order.

'Some people have called the *Experience of Bliss* the experience of Cosmic Consciousness. There are various levels – one is seeing the cosmos as one, or some level of ground which goes beyond the cosmos in time and space.

'Most people who have not been through this might say this is an illusion, might argue from the standpoint that it is a common illusion – e.g., there are people whose minds are disturbed who may engender these experiences. One has to look at all the possibilities. The commonness alone is not enough to prove it.

'What prevents it? If it is a real experience, then we must say it is a potential of all mankind. What is preventing it is the normal mode of consciousness, of thought which unfolds things as separate and treats that separateness as real. This is very much a second nature, this happens as a tendency. For some fortuitous reason it may be stopped for a while and for the same reason come back.

'Consciousness is a show; mind displays a kind of reality which is all unfolded. These displays do guide us in common activities correctly. It is a likeness of how things are, e.g., if I want to shave, I do not shave the image in the mirror. My activities are directed towards me. However, the image is still an image in the sense that it is a likeness of me. In that one part of me there is a part of the image. Beyond me is an image of what is not me. I see this as a faithful representation of me.

'When we think of an external object we make a similar display in the imagination – e.g., if you close your eyes and think of this room you may display it in front of you, if you noticed these things. Correctly or incorrectly. But you're separated.

'What about when a person tries to see a display [the outward, or unfolded image as opposed to the enfolded or implicate] of himself? He goes through what he calls introspection. Various images display themselves to him, seem to be happening inside – but I say these are not an image of *himself*. The image is the unfoldment of the display of *himself*. So the display in consciousness can be taken not for its content but rather to indicate the something inside (enfolded) which may not be functioning correctly.

'One could say that what one is conscious of inside can be a display of the actual activity of consciousness. Perhaps it might bring it to order.

'Evolution means to unfold. Evolution depends on being free from what is holding it back and this display displays what is holding it back and allows an activity to take place which will change that – illuminate it.

'If you remove the obstacle for a moment it unfolds, then comes back. The important thing is not merely to remove the obstacle but to see the obstacle, to be aware of the obstacle or for the obstacle to be aware of itself. So that it would not make an obstacle.'

'How is this going to change? It is necessary for people to see what is going on in consciousness. The activity which creates consciousness is not consciousness.

'Anything which goes wrong in consciousness is ultimately produced in the activity. But the activity is affected by the content because according to the content the activity takes place, so there is a back flow between them. This activity is not aware of itself and this is one of the difficulties.

'A major part of consciousness consists of the memory responding, to produce images and words, etc; e.g., if someone is angry it will leave a record of anger. Now, the memory of anger will not merely produce the pictures of what happens but all the chemical state of anger, so it *is* anger. The memory state of anger *is* anger. Then memory does not recognise that anger, which it has produced, as having been produced by it [self] but treats it [anger] as independent, and we say "That's me being angry". Memory is not able to do anything about anger because it is now controlled by anger. Once there is anger there, that chemical state will distort the consciousness and make thoughts which sustain the anger, like jealousy, fear, hatred.

'. . .[Sometimes] people in order to think pleasant thoughts, accept [as true] things that are false. I think it is a problem that is facing mankind now; we have a primitive way of thinking which really goes back to the stone age, and was alright for the stone age but is too dangerous to be carried out now. For example, if people from different nations, religions, sit down to discuss all this, chemistry goes into play and then nothing more can be done. It does not seem this can go for another hundred or thousand years, something will surely snap somewhere. Something is needed to break through . . . But I don't think mystic experience will affect practical people, politicians, for a long time.

'I don't want to say that mystic experience could be a glimpse of the reality that could sweep away the obstacles (the display), nor to claim that ultimately the reality is in the enfolded order. This might not necessarily be true . . .

'But – it is a possibility.'

Harmonising the measurable and the immeasurable

David Bohm is a scientist, but he does not draw a rigid line between physics and metaphysics in his search for answers. He has delved into Eastern philosophy, and entered into dialogue with such spiritual teachers as Krishnamurti on the ultimate nature of consciousness. He believes that 'fragmentation' is at the heart of the difference between the philosophies of East and West, that Western science concentrates on the measure of things in separate contexts, thereby missing their interdependent or interfused wholeness, whereas the East has always considered wholeness, the immeasurable, as reality. He says:

'It is of course impossible to go back to a state of wholeness that may have been present before the split between East and West developed (if only because we know little, if anything, about this state). Rather, what is needed is to learn afresh, to observe, and to discover for ourselves the meaning of wholeness....

'Actually, there are no direct and positive things that man can do to get in touch with the immeasurable, for this must be immensely beyond anything that man can grasp with his mind or accomplish with his hands or his instruments.

'What man *can* do is to give his full attention and creative energies to bring clarity and order into the totality of the field of measure [i.e. those things which are not immeasurable]. This involves, of course, not only the outward display of measure in terms of external units, but also inward measure, as health of the body, moderation in action, and meditation, which gives insight into the measure of thought...Such insight implies an original and creative act of perception into all aspects of life, mental and physical, both through the senses and through the mind, and this is perhaps the true meaning of meditation.'

Since fragmentation and fixed forms of measure lead to generally mechanical, routinized and habitual modes of thought, they eventually cease to be adequate and lead to 'forms of unclarity and confusion'.

'However, when the whole field of measure is open to original and creative insight, without any fixed limits or barriers, then our overall world views will cease to be rigid, and the whole field of measure will come into harmony...

'But – original and creative insight within the whole field of measure *is* the action of the immeasurable. For when such insight occurs, the source cannot be within ideas already contained in the field of measure but rather has to be in the immeasurable, which contains the essential formative cause of all that happens in the field of measure. The measurable and the immeasurable are then in harmony and indeed one sees that they are but different ways of considering the one and undivided whole.

'When such harmony prevails, man can then not only have insight into the meaning of wholeness but, what is much more significant, he can realise the truth of this insight in every phase and aspect of his life.

'As Krishnamurti has brought out with great force and clarity, this requires that man gives his full creative energies to the inquiry into the whole field of measure. To do this may perhaps be extremely difficult and arduous, but since everything turns on this, it is surely worthy of the serious attention and utmost consideration of each of us.'

Bliss, the New Physics and Ecology

'...Ever since the "quantum revolution" of fifty years ago various physicists have been finding intriguing parallels between their results and certain mystical-transcendental religions' – Ken Wilber, *The Holographic Paradigm – and other paradoxes* (1982)

With his widely-read book, *The Tao of Physics*, first published in 1975, Fritjof Capra, a research physicist currently lecturing at the University of California, Berkeley, undertook to explore the possible interrelation between the underlying concepts of modern physics and the basic ideas of Eastern mysticism.

In a paper presented at a Wrekin Trust Lecture at King's College, Winchester in 1978, Fritjof Capra gave an overview of these parallels:

'To begin with, let me briefly describe the world view which was changed by the discoveries of modern physics. This view had been a mechanistic view of the world. It had its roots in the philosophy of the Greek atomists who saw matter as being made of several "basic building blocks", the atoms, which are purely passive and intrinsically dead. They were thought to be moved by some external force which was often assumed to be of spiritual origin, and thus fundamentally different from matter.

'This image became an essential part of the Western way of thinking. It gave rise to the dualism between spirit and matter, between the mind and the body, which is characteristic of Western thought. This dualism was formulated in its sharpest form in the philosophy of Descartes who based his view of nature on the fundamental division between spirit and matter, between the 'I' and the world...Such a mechanistic world view was held by Newton who constructed his mechanics on its basis and made it the foundation of classical physics. From the second half of the 17th century to the end of the 19th, the mechanistic Newtonian model of the universe dominated all scientific thought.

'In contrast to the mechanistic view, the Eastern view of the world is an "organic" one. For the Eastern mystic, all things and phenomena we perceive with our senses are interrelated, are connected, and are but different aspects or manifestations of the same ultimate reality. Our tendency to divide the perceived world into individual and separate things and to experience ourselves as isolated egos in this world is seen as an illusion which comes from our measuring and categorising mentality. . . . The cosmos is seen as one inseparable reality which is forever in motion, alive, organic; spiritual and material at the same time. I shall now try to show how the main features of this picture appear in modern physics.

'At the beginning of our century, the experimental investigation of atoms gave sensational and totally unexpected results. Far from being the hard and solid particles they were believed to be since antiquity, the atoms turned out to consist of vast regions of empty space in which extremely small particles – the electrons – moved around the nucleus.

'When quantum theory, the theoretical foundation of atomic physics, was worked out in the 1920's, it became clear that even the subatomic particles, i.e., the electrons and the protons and neutrons in the nucleus, were nothing like the solid objects of classical physics. The subatomic units of matter are very abstract entities. Depending on how we look at them, they appear sometimes as particles, sometimes as waves. This dual aspect of matter was extremely puzzling. The picture of a wave which is always spread out in space is fundamentally different from the particle picture which implies a sharp location.

'The apparent contradiction between the two pictures was finally solved in a completely unexpected way which gave a blow to the very foundation of the mechanistic world view, to the concept of the reality of matter. At the subatomic level, matter does not exist with certainty at definite places, but rather shows "tendencies to exist".

'These tendencies are expressed, in quantum theory, as probabilities and the corresponding mathematical quantities take the form of waves. This is why particles can be waves at the same time. They are not "real" three-dimensional waves like sound or water waves. They are "probability waves", abstract mathematical quantities with all the characteristic properties of waves which are related to the probabilities of finding the particles at particular points in space and at particular times.

'It is important to realise that the statistical formulation of the laws of atomic and subatomic physics does not reflect our ignorance of the physical situation, like the use of probabilities by insurance companies or gamblers. In quantum theory, we have come to recognise probability as a fundamental feature of the atomic reality which governs all atomic and subatomic phenomena.

'This fundamental role of probability implies a new notion of causality. In quantum theory, individual events do not have a well-defined cause. For example, the jump of an electron from one atomic orbit to the other, or the disintegration of a subatomic particle, will occur spontaneously without any single event causing it. We can only predict the probability for the event to happen.

'This does not mean that atomic events occur in completely arbitrary fashion; they are governed by statistical laws. The narrow classical notion of causality is thus replaced by the wider concept of statistical causality in which the probabilities for atomic events are determined by the dynamics of the whole system.

The cosmic web

'At the atomic level, then, the solid material objects of classical physics dissolve into wave-like patterns of probabilities. These patterns, further-more, do not represent probabilities of things, but rather probabilities of inter-connections. A careful analysis of the process of observation in atomic physics shows that the subatomic particles have no meaning as isolated entities, but can only be understood as interconnections between the preparation of an experiment and the subsequent measurement. Subatomic particles are not "things" but interconnections between things, and these "things" are interconnections between other things, and so on.

'In atomic physics, you never end up with any "things" at all; you always end up with inter-connections.

'This is how quantum theory reveals a basic oneness of the universe. It shows that we cannot decompose the world into independently existing smallest units. As we penetrate into matter, nature does not show us any isolated building blocks, but rather appears as a complicated web of relations between the various parts of a unified whole. In the words of Werner Heisenberg: "The world thus appears as a complicated tissue of events, in which connections of different kinds alternate or overlap or combine and thereby determine the texture of the whole."

'This, however, is the way in which the Eastern mystics experience the world, and they often express their experience in words which are almost identical to the words used by atomic physicists. Take, for example, the following quotation from a Tibetan Buddhist, Lama Govinda: "The external world and his inner world are for [the Buddhist] only two sides of the same fabric, in which the threads of all forces and of all events, of all forms of consciousness and of their objects, are woven into an inseparable net of endless, mutually conditioned relations."

'These words by Lama Govinda bring out another feature which is of fundamental importance both in modern physics and in Eastern mysticism. The universal interconnectedness of nature always includes the human observer and his or her consciousness in an essential way. In quantum theory, the observed "objects" can only be understood in terms of the interaction between the processes of preparation and measurement, and the end of this chain of processes lies always in the consciousness of the human observer.

'The crucial feature of quantum theory is that the human observer is not only necessary to observe the properties of an object, but is necessary even to bring about these properties. My conscious decision about how to observe, say, an electron – whether I decide to use my apparatus in one way or another – will determine the electron's properties to some extent. In other words, *the electron does not have objective properties independent of my mind.* In atomic physics, the sharp Cartesian split between mind and matter, between the I and the world, is no longer valid. We can never speak about nature without, at the same time, speaking about ourselves. In the words of Heisenberg: "Natural science does not simply describe and explain nature; it is a part of the interplay between nature and ourselves."

'In modern physics, then, the scientist cannot play the role of a detached observer, but gets involved in the world he or she observes . . . . Participates. The notion of the participator is thus basic to the mystical traditions of the Far East.

' . . . . It is fascinating to see that the idea of each particle [outlined in the paper as Restlessness of Matter, the Relativity Theory, 'The Bootstrap Idea' that nature cannot be reduced to fundamental entities, and the Hadron Bootstrap, describing the 'dynamic "space-time" patterns which do not "contain" one another but rather involve one another in mathematical meaning not easily expressed in words'] containing all the others has also arisen in Eastern mysticism. It is to be found in Mahayana Buddhism where it is known as "interpenetration". In the words of D.T. Suzuki, "When the one is set against all the others, the one is seen as pervading them all and at the same time embracing them all in itself."

'This concept is illustrated in Buddhist texts by many parables. Here is one of them which uses the image of a network of pearls to illustrate the idea of the interconnected web: "In the heaven of Indra, there is said to be a network of pearls, so arranged that if you look at one you see all the others reflected in it. In the same way each object in the world is not merely itself but involves every other object and in fact *is* everything else:"

'The similarity of this image with . . . The bootstrap idea [in particle physics] of an interconnected web of relations, in which particles are dynamically composed of one another, represents the culmination of a view of nature that arose in quantum theory with the realisation of an essential inter-connectedness, and was further shaped by relativity theory when it was recognised that the cosmic web is intrinsically dynamic; that its activity is the very essence of its being.

'At the same time, this view of nature came ever closer to the Eastern world view and is now, with this current theory, in harmony with Eastern mysticism both in its general philosophy and in its specific picture of matter.'

In the Epilogue of his book *The Tao of Physics*, Fritjof Capra concludes: 'Once these parallels between Western science and Eastern mysticism are accepted, a number of questions will arise concerning their implications. Is modern science, with all its sophisticated machinery, merely redis-covering ancient wisdom, known to the Eastern sages for thousands of years? Should physicists, therefore, abandon the scientific method and begin to meditate? Or can there be a mutual influence between science and mysticism; perhaps even a synthesis?

'I think all these questions have to be answered in the negative. I see science and mysticism as two complementary manifestations of the human mind; of its rational and intuitive faculties. The modern physicist experiences the world through an extreme specialization of the rational mind. The two approaches are entirely different and involve far more than a certain view of the physical world.

'However, they are complementary, as we have learned to say in physics. Neither is comprehended in the other, nor can either of them be reduced to the other, but both of them are necessary, supplementing one another for a fuller understanding of the world.

'To paraphrase an old Chinese saying, mystics understand the roots of the *Tao* but not its branches; scientists understand its branches but not its roots. Science does not need mysticism and mysticism does not need science, but man needs both. Mystic experience is necessary to understand the deepest nature of things, and science is essential for modern life. What we need, therefore, is not a synthesis but a dynamic interplay between mystical intuition and scientific analysis.'

He concludes with the observation that so far this has not been achieved in our society; mainly because despite the fact that their theories are leading to a world view that is similar to mysticism, 'it is striking how little this has affected the attitudes of most scientists'. To acquire mystic knowledge, he believes, 'means to undergo a transformation; one could even say that the knowledge *is* the transformation. Scientific knowledge, on the other hand, can often stay abstract and theoretical . . . today's physicists not only do not seem to realize the philosophical, cultural and spiritual implications of their theories, but actively support a society still based on the mechanistic world view . . . . To achieve a state of dynamic balance between the two views a radically different social and economic structure will be needed: a cultural revolution in the true sense of the word.'

The New Physics and the ineffable

In another study of these parallels, or complementary concepts, *The Dancing Wu Li Masters An Overview of the New Physics* (1979), Gary Zukav, himself not a physicist but an interested journalist, presents a further description of the subject for the layman. In particular, he shows how at the subatomic realm, physics departs from that which can be measured into the statistics of probability. Not only do waves and particles appear interchangeable, but they seem to know what they are doing, wherever they are, without any tangible means of message or signalling. How do they make this information transfer – or is it transferred at all?

In his final chapter *The End of Science*, Gary Zukav writes: 'There are several mutually exclusive possibilities. The first possibility . . . is that, appearances to the contrary, there really may be no such thing as "separate parts" in our world (in the dialect of physics, "locality fails"). In that case, the idea that events are autonomous happenings is an illusion. This would be the case for any "separate parts" that have interacted with each other at any time in the past. When "separate parts" interact with each other, they (their wave functions) become correlated through the exchange of conventional signals (forces).

'Unless this correlation is disrupted by other external forces, the wave functions representing these "separate parts" remain correlated forever. For such correlated "separate parts", what an experimenter does in this area has an intrinsic effect upon the results of an experiment in a distant, space-like separated area. This possibility entails a faster-than-light communication of a type different than conventional physics can explain.

'In this picture, what happens here is intimately and immediately connected to what happens elsewhere in the universe, and so on, simply because the "separate parts" of the universe are not separate parts.'

Gary Zukav makes a comparison here between Buddhist philosophy and *Tantra*: the first can be intellectualized – it is a function of the rational mind; the second transcends rationality. 'The most profound thinkers of the Indian civilization discovered that words and concepts could take them just so far – *Tantra*, which is a Sanskrit word meaning "to weave", is a practice, it has to be *done*.

'The development of Buddhism in India shows that a profound and penetrating intellectual quest into the ultimate nature of reality can culminate in, or at least set the stage for, a quantum leap beyond rationality.

'The development of physics in the twentieth century already has transformed the consciousness of those involved with it. The study of complementarity, the uncertainty principle, quantum field theory, and the Copenhagen Interpretation of Quantum Mechanics produces insights into the nature of reality very similar to those produced by the study of Eastern philosophy.' Through the New Physics of this century, physicists have become increasingly aware that they are confronting the ineffable. Gary Zukav then quotes Professor G.F. Chew, Chairman of the Physics Department at Berkeley University, California:

'Our current struggle with (certain aspects of advanced physics) may thus be only a foretaste of a completely new form of human intellectual endeavor, one that will not only lie outside physics but will not even be describable as "scientific".

'We need not make a pilgrimage to India or Tibet. There is much to learn there, but here at home, in the most inconceivable of places, amidst the particle accelerators and computers, our own Path without Form is emerging.'

Similar theories from a slightly different view are contributed here by Fred Alan Wolf, a theoretical physicist of San Diego University, California who also worked alongside David Bohm at Birkbeck College and wrote *Taking the Quantum Leap*:

'In *Leap* I hinted at the idea that quantum physics and human consciousness were intimately related. The basis for this is the role of the observer in the act of observation. The observer is not passive. Instead, the observer plays a unique role. This role depends on what the observer believes is out there. (If one looks for waves one finds waves, if one looks for particles one finds particles.)

'Thus humans play a far greater role in their own destinies than they may have originally thought. Indeed we seem to be "ruled" by our own projections of what is and what isn't. In other words we live by our wits in the sense that we project our abstractions into the physical world. An example is the concept of the "state".

'The "state" is pure abstraction. Yet we all believe in it and in its power to rule over us. We create physical buildings – state Capitols, etc., that embody the "state". We feel imprisoned by it, etc. Thus our abstraction takes on a superlife of its own. Doesn't it follow that we can create, through our acts of observation, the "bliss state?"